THE TROJAN WOMEN

ANOTHER TRANSLATION
BY HOWARD RUBENSTEIN

AGAMEMNON: A Play by Aeschylus (ISBN 0-9638886-4-1)
Granite Hills Press™, 1998

"lively . . . vigorous . . . great directness . . . accessible to modern audiences"
—P. E. Easterling
Regius Professor of Greek
University of Cambridge, England

"vivid and immediate"
—Oliver Taplin
Professor of Classical Languages and Literature
University of Oxford, England

A videotape of the Granite Hills Acting Workshop's 1997 performance of the Rubenstein translation of *AGAMEMNON* has been placed in the Archive of Performances of Greek and Roman Drama, University of Oxford, England.

ABOUT THE AUTHOR

HOWARD RUBENSTEIN was born in 1931 in Chicago, where he attended Lake View High School. He was a *magna cum laude* graduate of Carleton College, where he was elected to Phi Beta Kappa and Sigma Xi and won the Noyes Prize for excellence in Greek studies. Rubenstein received his M.D. degree from the Harvard Medical School and has been a physician for over forty years, most of them at Harvard University. He has published many articles and is the author of several books. Now retired from the practice of medicine, he lives with his wife, Judy, in rural San Diego County, where he writes and gardens. The Rubensteins have four grown children.

THE TROJAN WOMEN

A Play by EURIPIDES

Translated from the Greek into English and

Adapted

in Response to
Aristophanes' and Aristotle's Criticism

by

HOWARD RUBENSTEIN

Granite Hills Press™
El Cajon, California

THE TROJAN WOMEN
A Play by EURIPIDES
Translated from the Greek into English and
Adapted
in Response to Aristophanes' and Aristotle's Criticism
by Howard Rubenstein

Cover: design by Douglas Miller, computer graphics by Lynn Hill, cyberwatercolor based on a detail of a photo, used by permission, by Barry Bosworth of a scene from the Granite Hills Acting Workshop's production of *The Trojan Women*, March 2001.

Published by Granite Hills Press™
P.O. Box P, El Cajon, CA 92022 USA
Tel: (619) 442-0056; Fax: (619) 442-2392
e-mail: ghp@granitehillspress.com
SAN 298-072X

First Edition 2002   ISBN 1-929468-05-9
Library of Congress Control Number: 2001135367
Printed in the USA

Publisher's Cataloging-in-Publication Data
Euripides.
    [Trojan women. English]
    The Trojan women : a play / by Euripides ; translated
from the Greek into English and adapted in response to
Aristophanes' and Aristotle's criticism by Howard
Rubenstein. -- 1st ed.
    p. cm.
    Includes bibliographical references.
    LCCN: 2001135367
    ISBN: 1-929468-05-9

    1. Hecuba (Legendary character)--Drama. 2. Helen of
Troy (Greek mythology)--Drama. 3. Queens--Troy (Extinct
city)--Drama. 4. Trojan War--Drama. 5. Tragedies.
I. Rubenstein, Howard S., 1931- II. Title.

PA3975.T8.R83 2002   882'.01
                            QBI01-201299

To Judy

CONTENTS

ACKNOWLEDGMENTS

I am indebted to many teachers and scholars for help and inspiration in translating and adapting Euripides' *The Trojan Women*. First, I am grateful to my high school Latin teacher, Genevieve Souther, Lake View High School, Chicago, who kindled in me a love of classical literature. Next, I am indebted to Charles Rayment, professor of Greek, Carleton College, Northfield, Minnesota, who taught me classical Greek and thereby made ancient Greek literature accessible to me.

In translating *The Trojan Women*, I made use of two Greek texts, the "eclectic" text in the Loeb Classical Library (1912, 1959) and the "Oxford" text in Barlow (1981, 1986, 1993). The English translations that were most useful to me were those by Gilbert Murray, Edith Hamilton, and Shirley Barlow.

I am indebted to the comic playwright Aristophanes for his literary criticism of Euripides in his comedies, particularly *The Frogs*, and to the philosopher Aristotle for his literary criticism of Euripides in his essay *Poetics*. I responded to the criticism I considered valid today (see Introduction) and thereby transformed my translation into an adaptation which I believe better serves a modern audience.

I thank Mary Brandes, Susan Rubenstein, Carol Ganzel, and Rebecca Rauff for their thoughtful editing of at least one draft of the manuscript.

I am particularly indebted to Barry Bosworth, director of the Granite Hills Acting Workshop of Granite Hills High School, El Cajon, California, for staging the premiere of this adaptation in February and March 2001 and for his intelligent and creative direction. The questions that he and the actors raised about the translation contributed to its clarification. Bosworth changed some of my stage directions and invented others, many of which I gratefully incorporated in this adaptation.

Above all, I thank my wife, Judy, who edited all drafts of the manuscript, asked many questions that required answers, made many suggestions, and helped solve many puzzles. Without her help, understanding, persistence, and patience, this adaptation would not have been completed, produced, or published.

Although I cannot adequately thank all the people who helped me in writing this book, I take sole responsibility for any errors it may contain.

INTRODUCTION

The Trojan Women by Euripides was first produced in 415 B.C. at the major dramatic festival and competition held annually in Athens. It was the third play in a trilogy, the first and second plays of which have been lost, but, like other plays in trilogies, *The Trojan Women* is a complete play in itself. Euripides' trilogy won second prize. First prize went to a playwright about whom nothing is known and whose work has not survived.

Oates and O'Neill (9, p. 958) state that regarding the "cruelty, folly, and futility of war, European literature can boast a no more potent document . . . than *The Trojan Women.*" Easterling (6, p. 82) says *The Trojan Women* is "the most vivid tableau of war's terror and cruelty." Hamilton (10, p. 19) asserts that *The Trojan Women* is the "greatest piece of anti-war literature there is in the world." Murray (15, p. 67) intimates that *The Trojan Women*, in addition to being the greatest of anti-war plays, may also be the greatest of tragedies because it contains scenes that are "perhaps the most absolutely heart-rending in all the tragic literature of the world. After rising from [a performance of *The Trojan Women*] one understands Aristotle's judgment of Euripides as 'the most tragic of the poets.'"

Perhaps if a theater company in every major city of the world were to produce *The Trojan Women* at least once a year, we might be closer to establishing world peace.

SYNOPSIS

The Trojan Women begins a day or so after the end of the Trojan War. The Greeks are victorious. They have killed the Trojan men and have captured and enslaved the Trojan women and children. The scene is a prisoner-of-war camp where the Greeks are holding selected Trojan women. The ordinary or non-selected Trojan women are alluded to but are not characters in the play. They are in camps elsewhere on the Trojan plain and have been assigned to the ordinary Greek soldiers randomly by lot. However, each woman in this camp has been specifically selected by a Greek leader for himself, but at the play's onset the women do not know they have been selected. (This selection process is frequently called in Greek literature "a gift from the army" because the leader indicated his choice and then the army assented or "gave" his choice to him.)

The women lament their loss of Troy and of everyone and everything they hold dear. They relate how the Greeks massacred the Trojan men and terrorized the populace. They express anxiety and fear of the unknown fate that awaits them. Each wonders which Greek leader will be her new master and to what part of Greece she will be taken in one of the Greek ships anchored in the Trojan harbor. While the women wait, they learn and witness things that increase their pain and loss. By the time the play ends, Troy itself has physically fallen, and the last prince of Troy, a little boy, has been murdered.

The play has six major interactions—each a variation on the theme of the loss of Troy. Five of the interactions are closely related in content. They are, in order, between the following characters:

Hecuba, the queen of Troy, and the Chorus of Trojan women;

Hecuba and her daughter Cassandra, a princess and prophet of Troy, who is about to become the bride of King Agamemnon, the commander in chief of all the conquering Greek forces;

Hecuba and her daughter-in-law Andromache (widow of Hector, the commander in chief of all the Trojans), who is about to become the bride of Pyrrhus, the son of Achilles, the Greek warrior who killed Hector;

Andromache and her son, Astyanax, the only surviving prince of Troy, who is sentenced to death by the Greeks because he is the son of Hector and therefore a potential threat to Greece; and

Hecuba and the corpse of Astyanax, her dead grandson, whose death symbolizes to the Trojan women the extinction of the Trojan people.

The sixth interaction (which comes fifth in the play) is between Hecuba, King Menelaus of Greece, and Helen, the unfaithful wife of Menelaus. This interaction differs from the others in two respects: it is comic as well as serious, and it focuses on Helen's elopement with Paris, a prince of Troy; this elopement is the cause of the Trojan War and the source of the troubles described in the other five interactions.

Another character in the play, the Greek herald Talthybius, is interwoven through all the interactions except the one between Hecuba, Menelaus, and Helen. Talthybius gives the point of view of the Greek enemy and particularly an ordinary soldier, thereby contrasting and balancing the views expressed by the Trojan women. Moreover, his viewpoint is that of a humane Greek. Although he is a dutiful soldier who carries out orders efficiently and effectively, he has strong opinions and feelings. He is intelligent, wise, and surprisingly kind.

Although Menelaus, like Talthybius, expresses views of the Greek enemy and also contrasts with the views expressed by the Trojan women, Menelaus' point of view is different from that of Talthybius for several reasons: Menelaus is royalty and a Greek general. He is highly focused on Helen, his wife, rather than on war, its horrors, and its consequences. Although Menelaus is a king, he is weak of will, easily manipulated, of limited intelligence, and only minimally aware of his own feelings. He is also a bit of a buffoon.

In between the interactions of the main characters, the Chorus chants choral odes. The most beautiful and dramatic of these concerns the Trojan Horse, the trick by which the Greeks entered and conquered Troy.

I suggest that the form of this play is a theme and variations. This form is well known in music but is rare, if not unique, in tragedy. Despite its recurrent themes, *The Trojan Women* has a progressive and dramatic development similar to certain musical compositions of this form, notably, Bach's *Passacaglia in C Minor for Organ* and Ravel's *Bolero*.

QUOTATIONS

All quotations from the play *The Trojan Women* are from this adaptation. Line numbers apply to the Greek text and page numbers to the pages in this adaptation (see Note 1).

Quotations from sources other than the play come from references listed in the Selected Sources. Scientific reference format (source number and page) has been used for simplicity.

Many of the quotations involve multiple sentences, phrases, and ellipses. Ellipsis dots and brackets to enclose equivalent words or phrases are used in the conventional way. But the use of brackets to indicate a change in capitalization from the original has been avoided to enhance readability and clarity. For example, "[T]he" is given as "The." In no instance does the altered capitalization change the meaning of the quoted text.

LIFE OF EURIPIDES

Of the three great Greek tragedians—Aeschylus (c. 525–c. 455 B.C.), Sophocles (c. 496–406 B.C.), and Euripides (c. 482–406 B.C.)—Euripides is the most contemporary to us, not only in time but also in spirit.

Much so-called information regarding Euripides' life comes from unreliable sources—biographers who lived two or more centuries after his birth. These biographers valued only the wellborn (*eugenia*) and some asserted that

Euripides came from a wellborn family.   However, the writings of Euripides' younger contemporary, the comic playwright Aristophanes (c. 450–388 B.C.), indicate that Euripides came from a humble family. Similarly, the biographers said that Euripides was universally loved in his day, but evidence from his contemporary Aristophanes and from his own plays indicates that he was not universally loved.

Aristophanes ridiculed Euripides incessantly for many reasons but especially for his family's poverty and low social class.   Aristophanes told us repeatedly that Euripides' mother sold vegetables in the marketplace, a particularly low class occupation at that time.   In Aristophanes' comedy *The Frogs*, the character Euripides says, "My first appearing character explained . . . the whole play's pedigree."   To this, another character retorts, "Your own you left in wise obscurity!" (3, p. 968). That Euripides was bothered by such derision is suggested by his own play *Melanippe*, in which a character says, "My spirit loathes these mockers whose unbridled mockery invades grave themes" (13, p. 901).

Although many of the details surrounding Euripides' life are unknown, and almost nothing is known about Euripides' father, scholars believe that Euripides probably was born near Athens, that he was married twice, and that his second wife was the mother of his three sons. Aristophanes in *The Frogs* perpetuated a rumor that at least one of his wives was unfaithful to him.

Scholars believe that Euripides began to write plays at about the age of twenty and that he entered his first competition in his mid-twenties with *The Daughters of Pelias*, which has not survived. Thereafter, writing tragedies became his life's work. He wrote between seventy-five and ninety-two plays, of which nineteen have survived. Euripides' most famous surviving plays are the following four: *Hippolytus* (the second of two versions survives; neither won a prize), *Medea* (which won third prize), *Bacchae* (which won first prize posthumously), and *The Trojan Women* (which won second prize).

Euripides won first prize at the annual Athenian dramatic competition only four times while he lived. None of those plays has survived. None of his famous extant plays won first prize while he lived.

By comparison, Aeschylus wrote about eighty plays and won first prize about twenty times. Sophocles wrote 125 or so plays and also won about twenty first prizes. Evidently Euripides did not receive as much recognition and appreciation in his lifetime as Aeschylus and Sophocles did in theirs. The sources of Euripides' relative unpopularity with the Athenians may be the following:

First, Euripides expressed dissatisfaction with the usual portrayal of the Olympian gods. He stated that they needed to behave more morally and responsibly than human beings—not less so. In *The Trojan Women*, he repeatedly reminds us through Hecuba that the gods do not care about human suffering. These religious ideas were unsettling to his Athenian audience. (Even though he was speaking to Greeks of the ancient Greek religion, people of other religions may find his ideas no less unsettling today.) Although free speech was not explicitly forbidden in Athenian democracy, unpopular religious ideas were discussed at one's peril.

Second, Euripides was dissatisfied with Athenian democracy, which favored Athenians, men, the rich, the powerful, and the wellborn, and failed to acknowledge the dignity and worth of all human beings. His plays gave a powerful voice to those who had no voice and no power in Athenian democracy, such as women, strangers, the poor, and slaves.

Third, Euripides' ideas were too intellectual and philosophical for Athenian taste. During the fifth century B.C., philosophy was still in its infancy and was not yet warmly received in Athens. Even today intellectual ideas and philosophy remain the province of relatively few.

Fourth, Euripides did not participate in Athenian affairs. Athens expected civic participation by all its citizens, including playwrights. Aeschylus had fought at the battle of Marathon during the Persian Wars, and Sophocles was active in civic affairs. Euripides, however, preferred to spend his time in solitude, studying, thinking, and writing. His belief that this was a legitimate form of service to his nation is revealed in his play *Antiope* when a character says, "The quiet man is a source of safety for his friends and of great benefit to the city" (6, p. 68) and "If I can think straight, that is better than a powerful right arm" (6, p. 68). The Athenians were not impressed. They called Euripides "apathetic" and "indolent" (13, p. 902), and a legend developed that he wrote his plays in a cave on the island of Salamis, a derisive metaphor for his need for isolation.

In about 409 B.C., when Euripides was in his early seventies, he left Athens forever—apparently through self-imposed exile, perhaps encouraged by the establishment or because of his resentment at being underappreciated by his fellow Athenians. After stopping briefly in Thessaly, he continued on to Macedonia, where Greeks of distinction were always welcome. While living at the court of King Archelaus of Macedonia, Euripides wrote his last play—one of his most famous—*Bacchae*, which means "the female followers of Bacchus." (Bacchus is an alternative Greek name for the god Dionysus as well as the Latin name for the same god.)

Euripides died in exile in Macedonia in 406 B.C. When Sophocles, who was in the process of producing one of his own plays, heard of Euripides' death, he instructed the actors to appear in clothes of mourning rather than in costume. This tribute by Sophocles was rare, if not unique, among Euripides' contemporaries. Posterity, however, has judged Euripides more favorably. Today critics and scholars consider Euripides the most modern of the three great tragedians of ancient Greece, and his plays are revived and performed the most frequently (5, p. 225).

SOURCES AND RELIGIOUS PHILOSOPHY

Euripides relied largely upon Homer and dealt with many of the same mythological characters and themes as Homer did, but he used other sources as well. Like

Aeschylus before him, he often changed the stories to suit his needs.

Aeschylus, the father of Greek tragedy, was born two generations earlier than Euripides. Aeschylus displayed a profound understanding of human psychology, gave dignity to people on all levels of society, recognized the dilemmas of the human condition, questioned the gods as portrayed in the traditional Greek religion, and condemned the Trojan War, all in magnificent poetry. Euripides developed and extended these themes, but in poetry crafted from ordinary language.

Euripides, in his plays, teaches people to question everything and to think for themselves. Significantly, these two teachings constitute the core of Socratic philosophy. According to legend, Socrates (c. 470–399 B.C.) was so fond of plays by Euripides that he would walk great distances to see one, but he would not see plays by other authors (15, p. 12). Another legend says that Socrates and Euripides were friends. These two legends and the common teachings of the two men imply that Socrates and Euripides had a profound influence upon one another.

Euripides' plays show a religious philosophy that changed throughout his lifetime. For the most part he portrays the immortal gods as Homer did—as vain, self-indulgent, indifferent to human suffering, and even at times cruel. However, he also says that the gods do not— or should not—behave in this manner. For example, in *The Trojan Women*, the character Helen tells the traditional mythological story of the beauty contest between three goddesses. In contrast, the character Hecuba disdains the myth on the grounds that the gods are not concerned with their own beauty. In Euripides' play *Heracles*, a character condemns Zeus thus: "You are a callous, ignorant god— or else there is no justice in your nature" (6, p. 69). Cadmus, a character in Euripides' *Bacchae*, says, "Gods should not be like mortals in their passions" (6, p. 69).

In *The Trojan Women*, Euripides speaks of the traditional sacrifice of Iphigenia to the goddess Artemis. But in his play *Iphigenia in Aulis*, the goddess Artemis rejects human sacrifice. And in his play *Heracles*, the title character says, "God, if he be God, lacketh naught" (15, p. 49). Gods who reject sacrifices are highly moral indeed.

Euripides also disdains prophecies and bird omens. In his play *Helen*, the herald says, "I realize how contemptible . . . are all the words of the prophets. So there was nothing sound in the voices of the fire oracle or the birds. Birds indeed—it was simple-minded to think that they were any use to men!" (6, p. 69). Even Cassandra, the greatest of the prophets outside of Delphi, does not entirely escape Euripides' scorn, as we shall see.

Aeschylus, in his play *Agamemnon*, saw divine purpose in human suffering and proposed that Zeus' great gift to mankind was teaching it that "wisdom comes through suffering" (1, p. 42). In contrast, Euripides found no purpose in human suffering and no wisdom to be gained from it. Nonetheless, in *The Trojan Women*, Euripides recognizes that there is an inexplicable human need to cry out to God in our suffering, even if God or the gods are indifferent to it—or could have prevented it—or may have caused it.

In *Bacchae*, a bizarre and horrifying play, Euripides portrays Dionysus, the new god of the mystery religion that is centered on him, as worse than any god Homer ever portrayed. This new god presents himself as gentle in temperament and soft and somewhat feminine in appearance, but he soon displays his true nature: he is fierce, savage, insatiable, and cruel—a deceiver and liar who relishes the degradation, humiliation, and murder of those who do not believe in him.

According to the mystery religion, Dionysus had made a secret promise, divulged on pain of death, that through the sacrament of drinking his blood or wine, his celebrants would be joined in a mystical union with him and thereby assured of everlasting life. Such a promise could not be kept secret for long. Although Euripides could not reveal the secret onstage, he knew that many in the audience were aware of it.

Bacchae is Euripides' last play. What is he saying in it? Is he celebrating the blessings of the mystery religion or showing it as evil and unworthy of people's worship, despite its famous promise? Aristophanes seems to hold the latter view. In his play *The Frogs*, the character Dionysus commands the character Euripides to burn incense to him, but Euripides refuses, responding, "The gods I pray to are of other metal!" (3, p. 966).

Today *Bacchae* remains a favorite of Greek scholars perhaps because it is the only extant Greek tragedy in which a god is the leading character, because it provides an in-depth portrayal and analysis of the god Dionysus, and because it contains some of Euripides' most admired poetry.

NEW CONCEPTIONS OF THE HEROIC

In the *Iliad*, Homer portrays men as heroic and glorious in battle. Away from the battlefield, however, these same glorious heroes reveal their ordinary humanity in some of the tenderest scenes in all literature. In these portrayals, Homer shows that heroes do not lose their heroism when they reveal their ordinary humanity; rather, they seem to enhance that heroism.

In *The Trojan Women*, Euripides goes beyond Homer by portraying the humanity not only of male heroes but also of ordinary men, women, slaves, and children, thereby giving dignity to all without discrimination. Euripides thereby teaches that all people are important and have important things to say. From his characters we learn that war is the concern not only of male heroes but also of these others, too. Thereby, Euripides expands the concept of the heroic.

Moreover, in *The Trojan Women*, Euripides teaches that even when people are knocked down as far as they can go—reduced to slavery—they must stand up and must endure. Euripides teaches, too, that even when people—whether royal or common—are physically vanquished, the human spirit is nonetheless invincible. Such heroism goes beyond that of Homeric heroes. Rarely if ever portrayed before, and certainly not with such intensity, this heroism may rightly be called "Euripidean." And Euripidean heroism is one of the characteristics that make Euripides modern.

MISOGYNIST OR FEMINIST?

Euripides has been described by some critics as a misogynist, by others as a feminist, but there is no evidence he was either. Misogyny is an aversion to women. Feminism is a political belief that women deserve the same rights as men, for example, in education, job opportunities, and suffrage.

As examples of Euripides' so-called misogyny, critics cite the character Phaedra in his play *Hippolytus* and the title character in his play *Medea.* Phaedra, the stepmother of Hippolytus, falls in love with him—with disastrous consequences. Medea is a scorned wife who murders her own children in order to get revenge on her husband.

Although ancient Athenians, and many people living today, would find a stepmother's erotic feelings toward her stepson and a mother's murder of her children disturbing, the portrayal of such sentiments and behavior onstage is not evidence of the playwright's misogyny. There are in the real world middle-aged women—stepmothers not excluded—who fall in love with young men, just as there are women who murder their children to punish unfaithful husbands. That Euripides wrote about such women shows not that he was a misogynist but that he was a realist who dared to show in his plays real feelings and real behavior, however unpleasant they might be and however uncomfortable they might make the audience. Such portrayals are examples of the psychological insights for which Euripides is famous. To modern audiences they are honest and highly believable.

Another example of Euripides' so-called misogyny is the declaration by the characters Hecuba and Menelaus in *The Trojan Women* that unfaithful wives deserve punishment by death. This declaration is entirely consistent with the beliefs of Hecuba and Menelaus, victims of Helen's infidelity. But the same point of view cannot be attributed to Euripides, even if, as rumored, his own wife was unfaithful. However, even if Euripides himself believed what Hecuba and Menelaus say, he cannot be singled out as a misogynist on the basis of this belief alone because female adultery was condemned by many in antiquity and is condemned by many today.

Euripides' "feminism" is no less debatable than his "misogyny." In Euripides' day, respectable Athenian women did not go outside their homes. (Athenian men—accompanied by slaves—did the marketing; it was no accident that the marketplace became such an important center for male-dominated government and business affairs.) In Euripides' play *Electra*, the title character goes outside the home. Is this an example of Euripides' feminism? Electra is married to a poor man. She *has to* go outside her home in order to fetch water. Electra's actions do not reveal any feminism on Euripides' part; they merely indicate that Electra could not afford to keep a slave to do the fetching for her. It was necessity—not feminism—that forced poor women to go outside the home and break this social norm. Euripides knew this firsthand from observing his own mother.

In *The Trojan Women*, Andromache, who had been married to a prince and had been rich, boasts that she never went outside her home. Even so, she confides, she yearned to do so. Does Andromache's yearning indicate that Euripides was a feminist? Hardly, particularly when Andromache goes on to tell us she quashed those yearnings in order to be a respectable wife.

But Andromache does tell us something surprising. She says that at home, in a discussion with her husband, "I knew when it was right to have my own way and when it was right to yield to his wishes" (ll. 654–6, p. 102). Although this behavior may seem like the seed of feminism, especially when compared with more repressive cultures existing even today, this "feminism" is not specific to Euripides. Kitto states that Athenian women of the fifth century B.C. characteristically spoke up to their husbands at home. Kitto does not use as examples domestic matters but legal matters and current events (14, pp. 219–35). On reflection, these examples should not surprise us: Just listen to Hecuba and Andromache speak! Even if they lack the education of their husbands, they are clearly highly intelligent women with whom their husbands could carry on meaningful conversations and whose advice was worthy of their husbands' consideration. Yet these women do not speak of feminist issues as we understand them. This limited form of assertiveness shared by Athenian women of the fifth century B.C. can hardly be called feminism. On the other hand, there is abundant evidence that Euripides was concerned with human dignity for all members of society.

SOPHISTIC RHETORIC

Rhetoric was important to the ancient Greeks, as Homer tells us in the *Iliad* (Book 9, l. 443) where heroes were not only "doers of deeds" but also "speakers of speeches" (11, p. 415). Homer, for the most part however, was speaking of rhetoric based upon sound argument and reason; such rhetoric was articulate, clear, and pleasing. To use Homer's repeated metaphor, it flew on "words with wings."

Sophistic rhetoric, however, is altogether different. It is not based upon sound argument and reason. Sophistic rhetoric is the rhetoric of sophistry. It is the rhetoric of a specious argument. Sophistic rhetoric is the technique of using distortion and deception to enable a weak argument to triumph over a strong one by creating the illusion that the weaker argument *is* the stronger one. Sophistic rhetoric thereby undermines reason, particularly in a political or judicial or other intellectual process that depends upon the sound evaluation of competing arguments.

Sophistic rhetoric became popular in Greece in the late fifth century B.C. and remained so throughout the fourth. One can still observe it today throughout the world, particularly in the arguments of some lawyers or politicians.

Much Euripidean dialogue involves a courtroom-style debate in which both sides convincingly make their case. Euripides sometimes has one of the parties engage in sophistic rhetoric, and the audience may be taken in by it. Even when taken in, however, people are disquieted, for they know something is amiss even if they cannot identify what that something is.

Seeds of sophistic rhetoric are found in Homer as early as the eighth century B.C. For example, in the *Iliad* (Book 19, ll. 86–90), in the episode where Agamemnon and Achilles reconcile after their long quarrel, Agamemnon tries to absolve himself of all responsibility for his part in their quarrel by blaming his bad behavior on Zeus:

> It is not I that am at fault, but Zeus . . . [who] cast upon my soul fierce blindness. . . . But what could I do? It is God that bringeth all things to their issue (12, p. 343).

To make his case, Agamemnon uses absolute determinism, a philosophical system that does not allow any personal freedom or responsibility. Insofar as absolute determinism is an oversimplification, it is specious, and therefore a form of sophistic rhetoric.

Sophistic rhetoric is abundant in *The Trojan Women*. Helen appeals to her husband Menelaus for mercy (she thinks he plans to execute her). In her appeal, Helen sounds remarkably like Homer's Agamemnon. Helen readily admits that she is an adulteress but insists that she is not responsible for her adultery. It is Aphrodite, the Goddess of Love, who is responsible and should be blamed for Helen's bad behavior. Moreover, Helen argues, it is this very adultery that has enabled the Greeks to win the Trojan War. Helen, according to Helen, should therefore be praised, not blamed!

> Aphrodite's victory, which resulted in the marriage of Paris and me, brought great good to Greece, did it not? Greece has won the Trojan War. . . . But Greece's vic-

tory has ruined me. . . . I am reviled by the Greeks, from whom I ought to receive a crown. . . . Punish Aphrodite and forgive me! (ll. 932–50, pp. 129–31).

Her argument is irrefutable—except to those who see it for the hubristic nonsense it is. Euripides here either is using sophistic rhetoric as a device of humor or else—and it amounts to the same thing—he is ridiculing absolute determinism by showing that people can use it to escape personal responsibility and punishment for any crime.

Euripides uses sophistic rhetoric also in some of the speeches of Cassandra. For example, Cassandra says that she is going to prove that Troy, which has been annihilated, is more blessed than the Greeks who annihilated her. How, the audience asks itself, could that be possible? And yet, after listening to her arguments, one wonders if there might not be an element of truth in what she says. Moreover, near the end of the play, Hecuba voices a similar idea. Hecuba says that it is precisely because the gods are destroying Troy that Troy will give "everlasting themes in poetry and music to future generations" (l. 1245, p. 155). In other words, for the sake of Troy's immortality and future glory in literature, the destruction of Troy is a good thing!

Whatever truth there may be in this argument, it nonetheless remains a quintessential rationalization of the loser. For the larger truth of the matter is simply this: Greece won the Trojan War, and, however barbaric the Greeks may have been in winning it, they were the ones who wrote the glorious literature that describes the fall of Troy. Troy, on that subject, has been deathly silent.

Cassandra's analysis of Ulysses' fate is perhaps even more specious. Cassandra says that Ulysses, one solitary Greek, will suffer on his voyage home more than all the Trojans together suffered during the Trojan War. "All our troubles and all of Troy's will seem like gold compared to his" (l. 432, p. 82).

This is lunacy, but then Cassandra is insane. Ulysses, in the course of his long voyage home, has many adventures. Some of them are frightening and life-threatening, but most are exciting and wonderful, and he does eventually return home—and intact—to the waiting arms of a loving and faithful wife.

Euripides is surely telling us that it's no wonder Cassandra's prophesies are never believed, when she uses sophistic rhetoric. On the other hand, when Cassandra is sharing her wisdom rather than prophesying the future, she can be counted upon to be profoundly wise, as in the case of her opinion on the value of martial victory (see page 37).

Aristophanes ridicules Euripides' use of sophistic rhetoric. A character in *The Frogs* says that some of Euripides' characters opine, "Not to be living is truly to live!" (2, p. 399). Another character says on the same subject, "Who knows if death be life, and life be death, and breath be mutton broth, and sleep a sheepskin?" (2, p. 433).

Audiences are unsettled by sophistic rhetoric because they do not know where the playwright stands, and as a result they cannot use his position as a point of reference for their own. They feel confused. Confusion makes them question their own intelligence and powers of discrimination and makes them feel foolish. I suggest that the discomfort caused by Euripides' sophistic rhetoric is yet another reason why Euripides was not a favorite playwright of the ancient Athenians.

Modern audiences, however, are accustomed to becoming confused or unsettled and feeling foolish, whether through sophistic rhetoric or some other device of contortion in language or situation. Many modern playwrights, such as Pirandello, Beckett, Pinter, Stoppard, and Mamet, deliberately try to unsettle the audience. In attending a play by Euripides, then, a modern audience is seeing but another modern play. I suggest that familiarity with discomfort is another reason why modern audiences may react more favorably to Euripides than ancient audiences did. (To read more about sophistic rhetoric, see Simon Goldhill, in Easterling, 5, pp. 127–50.)

HUMOR

Although *The Trojan Women* is a tragedy, it contains moments of humor in addition to some of its sophistic rhetoric. A few examples follow:

The play contains probably the most famous one-liner joke in classical literature. When Hecuba tells Menelaus that he must not take Helen on board his ship, the context makes it clear that she is warning Menelaus not to set himself up for temptation lest his old love for Helen be reignited. But Menelaus responds ingenuously, "Why not? Has she gained weight?" (l. 1050, p. 140).

Much needed comic relief is provided by the entire episode between Helen, Menelaus, and Hecuba (ll. 895–1059, pp. 126–41). It is, therefore, essential that the actors cast for the parts of Helen and Menelaus be endowed with a touch of the comedian.

A more subtle type of humor emerges when the Trojan women try to imagine where in Greece they will be taken as slaves and by which leader. Several of the women express delight at the prospect of leaving Troy and going to a new land. One woman dreams of going to Sicily, where she has heard there exists a river whose waters turn brunettes to blondes or redheads. Some things never change! Another woman says she has heard that also in Sicily there are outstanding athletic contests. We suspect she is not so much interested in the contests as in the athletes. Another woman longs to go to the enemy's most famous city, Athens (ll. 207–29, pp. 64–5).

These examples may suggest that Euripides is poking fun at these women, and perhaps he is. More importantly, however, he is telling us, through humor, that the human spirit is resilient and full of hope even when the present is grim and the future uncertain. Moreover, some things, like the attraction between the sexes, override political boundaries. Additionally, in having the women praise Greece and the Greeks, perhaps Euripides was aware, long before the Stockholm effect was described in the late twentieth century, of the identification of the victim with the enemy upon whom she is dependent for survival. Perhaps, too, in praising Athens, Euripides was currying favor with the Athenian audience and critics and thinking about his own artistic survival as a playwright in Athens.

Even more subtle humor appears in Cassandra's torch scene. While talking about her forthcoming marriage to the man who has destroyed her nation, Cassandra does a mad bridal dance before her mother. Hecuba, embarrassed by this behavior, nonetheless makes a point of criticizing her, as mothers are wont to do, for not holding the torch upright! (l. 348, p. 75). This is comedy at its bitterest.

Aristophanes, the playwright of comedies, ridiculed Euripides incessantly; one reason, I suspect, was envy. Aristophanes realized that Euripides' humor was on a higher level than his own. Aristophanes typically caricatured current events and contemporaries, but his plots were thin, his character development slight, and his humor often gross. Many of his jokes are scatological and phallic, designed only to get a laugh. Scholars call Aristophanes' comedy the "old comedy."

In contrast, Euripides' humor is for the most part witty, intellectual, and part of the very fabric of his plays. Scholars see in Euripides' moments of comedy in his tragedies the forerunner of the "new comedy," in which plot and characters are integrated, dialogue contains a minimum of scatological and phallic jokes, and the laughter emerges largely from the context. This kind of comedy is characteristic of the Greek playwright Menander in the fourth century B.C., who influenced the Roman playwrights Plautus in the third century B.C. and Terence in the second century B.C. These two Roman playwrights in turn influenced almost all writers of comedy in the Western world to the present day. It is a supreme irony that modern comedy owes more to Euripides, a writer of tragedies, than to Aristophanes, a writer of comedies.

It would be helpful to educate the audience attending a performance of *The Trojan Women* regarding

Euripides' humor, perhaps in the program notes. Otherwise, on hearing in the audience the scattered laughter of the *cognoscenti* or those with an uninhibited and innate sense of humor, many in the audience may be puzzled and wonder, "This play is a tragedy. Why are those boors laughing?"

DICTION—COMMON LANGUAGE

In the poetry of his tragedies, Euripides used commonplace language, not the magnificent language of Aeschylus.   Kitto (15, p. vii) writes that Euripides' "poetry had none of Aeschylus' splendor or of Sophocles' dignity."   Whatever Euripides may lose in splendor or dignity, he gains in clarity of expression.   Clear expression of ideas in ordinary language is yet another reason Euripides is so modern.

ARISTOPHANES' AND ARISTOTLE'S CRITICISM OF EURIPIDES

Aristophanes (c. 450–388 B.C.), the writer of comedies and contemporary of Euripides, and Aristotle (384–322 B.C.), the philosopher who lived in the next century, provide the criticism of Euripides that survives from antiquity.

Six major criticisms of Euripides emerge from the collective writings of Aristophanes and Aristotle.   These two critics agree on two points: (1) Euripides' characters are not elevated nor enhanced; and (2) his choral odes are irrelevant to their context.

Three criticisms are made by Aristophanes alone: (3) Euripides is a man of humble origins in a society that values only the wellborn; (4) his prologues are defective; and (5) he tries to make people question everything and think for themselves, intellectual behaviors that disturb society.

One   criticism   is   made   by   Aristotle   alone: (6) Euripides created the *deus ex machina* (the god from the machine), a poor substitute for natural plot development.

Aristotle's criticism appears in his essay on literary criticism, *Poetics*. Aristophanes' criticism appears in his plays.   Murray (15, p. 13) asserts that Euripides is ridiculed in all eleven of Aristophanes' extant plays and that there is no parallel to such unrelenting ridicule of a fellow playwright "in all the history of literature" (15, p. 13). Aristophanes' literary criticism is especially concentrated in the final part of his play *The Frogs*.

The Frogs was first produced in 405 B.C., the year after Euripides and Sophocles died and fifty years after Aeschylus died.   Near the end of the play, which takes place in the underworld, the characters Euripides and Aeschylus engage in a fictional debate concerning which of them is the better playwright.   The character Sophocles refuses to participate in the debate because he has already decided that Aeschylus is the best of the three.   The outcome of the debate is that Aeschylus is declared the best playwright, Sophocles the second best.   Euripides, being so inferior, is not ranked.

Criticism 1. Characters Not Elevated Nor Enhanced (Shared by Aristophanes and Aristotle)

Both Aristophanes and Aristotle find it objectionable that Euripides did not enhance people's good characteristics and minimize their bad ones.   Both critics apparently expected Euripides to craft characters that were ideal and perfect, like the statues made by sculptors in the fifth century B.C.

Moreover,   instead   of   having   perfect   specimens, Euripides creates male characters who aren't even physically fit!   In *The Frogs*, a character says of some of Euripides characters, "But for wrestle or race not a muscle in trim! . . .   Why I laughed fit to cry . . . a man to espy, pale, flabby, and fat . . . and . . . puffing" (3, p. 975).

In fact, Euripides is the champion of the disabled.   In *The Frogs*, Aristophanes calls Euripides a "blind-beggar-bard and . . . crutch-and-cripple playwright" (3, p. 964). He notes that Euripides never writes of heroes who are "good six-footers, solid of limb, well-born, well-bred" (3, p. 971).   Aristophanes complains more.   "[Although the dress of heroes] must be gorgeous to view, and majestical, nothing like ours . . . [Euripides] came and spoilt it" (3, p. 974). Euripides "spoilt it" by writing of heroes dressed "in rags . . . to express their heroical woe" (3, p. 974). Moreover, Euripides' plays do not contain heroes who "hungered for havoc and gore. . . . to fight without flinching or fear. . . . [who long] for glory . . . and against all odds stand fast" (3, p. 972). In sum, Euripides' heroes, so often not physically fit, even disabled, in rags, not wellborn, or not well bred, do not glorify Greece.

Aristophanes complains that children as characters are as comfortable in the plays of Euripides as are strong men in the plays of others. "You have trained in the speech-making arts nigh every infant that crawls" (3, p. 974).

Aristophanes further complains that Euripides' characters speak openly and freely about their basest feelings, feelings best left unsaid. Regarding a stepmother's erotic love for her stepson, the character Euripides in *The Frogs* says, "But did I invent the story I told of Phaedra . . . ? Wasn't it history?" And a character responds, "It was true, right enough; but the poet should hold such a truth enveloped in mystery, and not represent it or make it a play" (3, p. 973).

Aristophanes complains that Euripides elevates not only the ordinary person but also the trivial topic; Euripides is not concerned with great subjects, great questions, and great themes, but composes a tragedy on any subject he chooses. He is a writer of "ugly amours" (3, p. 964). "What hasn't he done that is under the sun?" (3, p. 975). His concerns are ordinary, and his questions are as trivial as "Where is the saucepan gone?" or "Where are the leeks of yesterday?" or "Who has gnawed this olive, pray?" (3, p. 970).

The character Euripides responds to this criticism thus: "I put things on the stage that came from daily life . . . where men . . . could listen . . . to things they knew" (3, p. 969).

Aristophanes implies that in elevating the dregs of society and displaying their feelings and behavior, Euripides mocks Athenian democracy. From Aristophanes' criticism we may deduce that Athenian democracy of the fifth century B.C. was different from twenty-first-century A.D. Western democracy. In Athens in the fifth century B.C., women and the poor had no political voice, and slavery was legal. In *The Frogs*, the character Euripides proudly announces that characters from all walks of life appear in his plays: "The men, the slaves, the women, all made speeches, the kings, the little girls, the hags" (3, p. 968). One might add to the list, from the examples cited, the disabled, the destitute, the not wellborn, the not well bred, the physically deconditioned, and those harboring incestuous feelings. Another character asks in rebuttal, "And shouldn't you be hanged for that?" To which the character Euripides responds, "No, by the lord Apollo! It's democratic!" (3, p. 969). Euripides' concept of democracy was clearly more democratic than that of Athenian democracy. It was closer to Western democracy today.

Aristotle similarly criticizes Euripides for not enhancing people's good characteristics and minimizing their bad: "Poets should emulate good portrait painters, who render personal appearance and produce likenesses, yet enhance people's beauty" (4, p. 83). Aristotle supports his judgment by a statement he attributes to Sophocles: "Sophocles said he created characters as they ought to be, Euripides as they really are" (4, p. 129).

In short, Aristophanes and Aristotle criticize Euripides for creating plays with realistic characters. This negative evaluation of realistic characters has not stood the test of time. Modern critics and audiences do not find realistic portrayals a flaw but rather a strength. Realistic portrayals are yet another modern characteristic of Euripides.

Criticism 2. Choral Odes Irrelevant to Context (Shared by Aristophanes and Aristotle)

Aristophanes and Aristotle both criticize Euripides for writing choral odes or songs that are irrelevant to the context of the play. With the exception of the ode on the Ruse of the Trojan Horse in *The Trojan Women* and several of the odes in *Bacchae*, this criticism has merit. Jebb has written, "The choral songs in Euripides, it may be granted, have often nothing to do with the action" (13, p. 902).

Aristophanes has a character in *The Frogs* say, "Take [Euripides'] songs!" The character Euripides responds, "Wonderful songs they are! . . . I'll run them all together into one." A character replies, "But any place will d o " (3, pp. 983–5). Here Aristophanes is saying that the choral odes are so non-specific that Euripides could have placed any one of them anywhere in any of his plays.

Aristophanes also complains that Euripides' odes or songs are inappropriate. In *The Frogs*, the character Aeschylus says that Euripides, in the midst of serious subject matter, will suddenly sing about birds and spiders:

> 1) Ye halcyons by the dancing sea
> Who babble everlastingly . . .
>
> 2) And, oh, ye spiders deft to crawl
> In many a chink of roof and wall . . . (3, p. 985).

Aristotle, in a more straightforward way, also criticizes Euripides for the vagueness and non-specificity of the choral odes:

> The chorus should be treated as one of the actors; it
> should be a part of the whole and should participate, not
> as in Euripides but as in Sophocles (4, p. 95).

Aristotle is speaking in general terms about the Chorus. He does not discriminate between choral odes and choral dialogues. But he can have only the odes in mind because regarding the dialogues, the members of the Chorus *do* "participate" and their words *are* "part of the whole." For example, after Hecuba delivers a long and moving funeral oration over the dead prince, the Chorus Leader delivers two short sentences that distill the essence of Hecuba's speech and express the Chorus' own emotions: "My heart is breaking because of you. I hoped one day you'd be a great lord in our nation" (ll. 1216–18, p. 153). The other choral dialogues are no less participatory and no less part of the whole. Therefore, in this adaptation, there was no reason to change the choral dialogues. Regarding the choral odes, however, wherever I considered Aristophanes' and Aristotle's criticism valid, I changed the odes in order to make them relevant and "part of the whole" (see page 40).

Criticism 3. Humble Origins
(Aristophanes Alone)

Aristophanes criticizes Euripides for being a man of humble origins, a self-made man, which disqualifies him from serious consideration as a playwright. This evaluation is invalid today.

In four of the extant plays of Aristophanes (*The Acharnians*, *Knights*, *Thesmophoriazusae,* and especially *The Frogs*), he ridicules the lower-class social status of Euripides' mother, who sold vegetables in the marketplace. In *The Frogs*, a character contemptuously calls Euripides the "Son o' the Goddess of the Greens" (3, p. 964). In *The Acharnians*, a character sarcastically says to the character Euripides, "Give me some of the chervil your mother left you in her will" (3, p. 446). The character also says sarcastically, "May the gods grant you a destiny as brilliant as your mother's!" (3, p. 445).

Insulting Euripides by attacking his mother seems odd to us. Attacks on unskilled laborers are not funny today, particularly to those who value hard-working men or women in any honest line of work. But Athenians were not like us in this regard. Athenians admired only the wellborn. They scorned and ridiculed the poor. And in Athenian society, proper Greek women did not work (they had slaves for that purpose), nor did they go beyond the confines of their homes, except to go to the theater (14, pp. 219–35), apparently in the company of their husband or another woman.

The Athenians found Aristophanes' "little joke" about Euripides' poverty so funny that Aristophanes told it repeatedly. Murray (15, p. 13) observes, "The Athenian public never tired of this incessant . . . criticism in the midst of farce. . . . You cannot go on constantly deriding on the stage a person whom your audience does not wish derided."

In spite of its great contributions to humanity, ancient Greece had little to say on the subject of human dignity. Euripides may be unique in this regard. Euripides' acute sensitivity to human dignity probably stemmed from the fact that his mother had to sell vegetables in the market-place, a comic writer wrote about this as a joke, and Athenian audiences found the joke funny.

Aristophanes' negative evaluation of Euripides' humble origins has not stood the test of time. The self-made man is, in fact, an American ideal that modern audiences admire.

Criticism 4. Defective Prologues
(Aristophanes Alone)

Aristophanes found Euripides' prologues repetitious, padded, irrelevant, and filled with commonplace language and trivial objects such as cans of olive oil. In *The Frogs*, a characters says:

> You write [prologues with]
> The bed-quilt, or the oil-can, or the clothes-bag,
> All suit your tragic verse! (3, p. 980).

Then, to further prove his point, Aristophanes cites the prologues from several plays of Euripides in which the hero laments having lost his oil-can. Aristophanes' critique concludes, "They bristle with . . . oil-cans . . . your prologues" (3, p. 983).

Murray's own evaluation of Euripides' prologues is strikingly ambivalent. At first Murray seems as negative as Aristophanes: "At the very beginning of a play by Euripides we shall find something that seems deliberately calculated to offend us and destroy our interest: a Prologue ... The modern reader may [declare], 'The prologue is rather dull. It does not arrest the attention.'" Murray responds in agreement, "No; it does not" (15, pp. 104–5). The argument seems to end with a thunk.

Then Murray reverses himself and proceeds to justify Euripides' prologues: they quietly set the "atmosphere" with "something supernatural [and] something mysterious." They are "scenes of waiting, not acting—waiting till the atmosphere can slowly gain its full hold" (15, p. 106).

Apparently sensing that his mysterious explanation may not satisfy, Murray ends his discussion with a statement even more unsatisfying: "Certainly the prologue generally justifies itself in the acting" (15, p. 106). This argument is like saying that a play cannot be read but has to be acted in order to be appreciated, or that a great actor can make reading the telephone book an exciting piece of theater. This is hardly a defense of Euripides' prologues. Jebb has written that Euripides' prologues are "slipshod and sometimes ludicrous" (13, p. 902).

I confine my own judgment specifically to the prologue of *The Trojan Women*. There are many problems with this prologue. In it the gods Athena and Poseidon promise to raise a storm at sea to punish the Greeks as they sail home *after the play has ended* These gods, in effect, deliver an epilogue during the prologue. In addition, a storm at sea hardly seems adequate punishment for the destruction of Troy and the sacrileges the Greeks committed there. Moreover, we know from other sources that many well-known Greeks survived the storm, including Agamemnon, Menelaus, Helen, and Ulysses, so it is also likely that many ordinary Greeks survived. But even if the storm resulted in the drowning of a large number of Greeks, it also had to have drowned a proportionate number of Trojan women and children. How would a punitive storm on the Greeks that equally affected the Trojans be meaningful or effective?

Finally, by the end of *The Trojan Women*, most of the audience will have forgotten or will be unconcerned with a storm that begins after the play ends because the audience will be overwhelmingly unsettled and saddened by the death of Astyanax, the annihilation of Troy, and the march into slavery of the Trojan women. In sum, Aristophanes' criticism of Euripides' prologues is well supported by the prologue to *The Trojan Women*. Therefore, I have changed the Prologue in this adaptation (see page 40).

Criticism 5. Encouraging Questioning and Thinking (Aristophanes Alone)

Aristophanes says that Euripides encourages people to question everything and to think for themselves. To those of us living in a twenty-first-century Western democracy, this sounds like admiration, not condemnation. But in fifth-century B.C. Athens, this is harsh criticism indeed because these were seen as intellectual behaviors that disturbed society.

Aristophanes, in his comedy *The Frogs*, has the Chorus sing: "O blessed are they who . . . never [associate] with Socrates [and his] row of fools who gabble away . . . a-scraping of word on word, all idle and all absurd,—that is the fate of fools!" (3, pp. 993–4). Aristophanes' dim view of Socrates and philosophy is jarring to us, but in his day it was shared by the Athenians, who gave Socrates a choice of exile or death by suicide. Socrates chose death. Euripides, to our knowledge, was never tried in court, but he was harshly judged by his contemporaries. He chose exile. In his play *Medea*, the title character says, "If you introduce new, intelligent ideas to fools, you will be thought frivolous, not intelligent" (6, p. 65).

According to Aristophanes, before Euripides began writing plays, men accepted everything on blind faith like sheep and were happy because they didn't know any better, but Euripides changed all that. In *The Frogs*, the character Euripides says: "I taught all the town to talk with freedom. . . . [I] taught them to see, think, understand, to . . . question all things. . . ." A character responds, "'Twere better, ere you taught them, you had died amid their curses!" (3, p. 969).

The character Euripides also says, "I mingled reasoning with my art and shrewdness, till I fired their heart to brood, to think things through . . . and rule their houses better, too. . . ." To this a character observes, "[Before Euripides], each [person] sat at home, a simple, cool, religious, unsuspecting fool, and happy in his sheep-like way!" (3, p. 970).

Students at Western schools are told to think for themselves (even by teachers who don't really mean it). Most Westerners consider thinking for oneself admirable (even those who don't do it themselves). But in ancient Athens, thinking for oneself and encouraging others to do the same was a dangerous thing to do, as Socrates found out. Even today, in the twenty-first century, totalitarian political regimes and orthodox religions still condemn thinking for oneself. And even in English-speaking Western democracies, the word "freethinker" is still largely pejorative.

Nevertheless, within Western democracies, Aristophanes' negative evaluation of encouraging questioning and thinking has not triumphed, in spite of the many people who agree with his opinion. Indeed, encouraging questioning and independent thinking has helped advance civilization and is another characteristic of Euripides that makes him modern.

Criticism 6. The *Deus ex Machina* or the "God from the Machine"
(Aristotle Alone)

One of Aristotle's chief criticisms, which, curiously, Aristophanes does not mention, is the *deus ex machina* or the "god from the machine." Euripides often brought a god onstage on a crane-like device, which he seems to have been the first to use. Aristotle did not like the god from the machine, and neither do many modern commentators. (It is easy to imagine how Aristophanes might have made a hilarious parody of the god from a machine, but he did not do so, possibly because he did not want to be accused of ridiculing the gods.)

In common parlance today, a *deus ex machina* is a device that quickly resolves a situation that would, through ordinary means, take a long time to resolve, or it provides an escape where no escape seems possible.   However, Euripides' gods from the machine are different; they serve no useful purpose.   They do not resolve the plot or situation or do anything else functionally or artistically; they only intrude and detract.

The one apparent exception is the *deus ex machina* in *Medea*.   At the end of that play, the title character seems trapped until the sun god gives her his flying chariot with which to escape.   This seems like an authentic use of the *deus ex machina*—or at least one that fits our modern understanding of the phrase.

Aristotle, however, does not like it.   He writes, "Clearly the denouements of plots should issue from the plot as such, and not from a *deus ex machina* as in *Medea*" (4, p. 81).   Aristotle does not elaborate.   However, he probably means that the sun god and his flying chariot are unnecessary because Medea is a powerful enchantress who could create a flying chariot or some other escape device on her own.   If Euripides had had Medea escape through her own sorcery rather than through divine intervention by the *deus ex machina*, he would have crafted a better play.   Thus, the *deus ex machina* is unnecessary, even in *Medea*, and is a flaw in Euripides' craft.

Other plays of Euripides in which the *deus ex machina* is featured prominently are *Electra*, *Hippolytus*, *Rhesus*, and *Andromache* (15, p. 114).   To this list, I would add *The Trojan Women*.   In *The Trojan Women*, the gods Poseidon and Athena appear in the prologue, but scholars have not taken a stand as to how these gods enter and exit. Are they walk-on characters or are they gods from the machine?   Gods from the machine usually appear at the end of a play.   However, as mentioned earlier, the prologue of *The Trojan Women* is an epilogue in content.   I suggest that Euripides did not deliver the epilogue at the end of the play because the play's ending is awesome; and to place an epilogue there would ruin the dramatic effect.

Do gods at the beginning of a play become walk-on characters instead of gods from the machine just by virtue of their appearance at the beginning of the play? Conversely, do gods at the end of a play become gods from the machine instead of walk-on characters just by virtue of their appearance at the end of the play? There is no evidence to support either idea. In Euripides' play *Hippolytus*, the goddesses Aphrodite and Artemis are equally featured. Aphrodite appears at the beginning of the play, and Artemis at the end. Scholars agree that Artemis is a god from the machine, but they are curiously silent regarding Aphrodite, even though functionally Aphrodite is no different from Artemis.

Likewise, Poseidon and Athena in *The Trojan Women* are functionally no different from Aphrodite and Artemis in *Hippolytus*. The issue, as I see it, is not whether a god appears at the beginning or the end of a play. The issue is that a god's sudden and brief appearance in a play implies that the god just flew down from heaven or Mt. Olympus. To portray the god's flight and sudden appearance, a machine would be necessary, and that, I suggest, is the reason Euripides used it. But these gods with bit parts are unnecessary in Euripides' plays; therefore I agree with Aristotle's negative evaluation of the *deus ex machina*.

The only clear evidence in any of Euripides' plays of a walk-on god, for whom no machine would be necessary, is the character Dionysus in *Bacchae*. Dionysus is the protagonist. He does not make any sudden entrances or exits; moreover, the character is meant to walk among people.

Whether the gods in the prologue of *The Trojan Women* are gods from the machine or walk-on gods is, in the last analysis, moot. These gods and their message are unnecessary. Consequently I have deleted them from this adaptation (see page 40).

Aristophanes' Summation of Euripides

Aristophanes had five major criticisms of Euripides—characters not elevated nor enhanced, choral odes irrelevant to context, humble origins, defective prologues, and encouraging questioning and thinking. Therefore, it is not surprising to read Aristophanes' evaluation in *The Frogs* that Euripides' plays are so inferior that they died along with him: The character Aeschylus says, "My writings haven't died with me, as [Euripides'] have" (3, p. 965).

Unlike Aristotle, who would follow him in the next century, Aristophanes does not make any explicit statements about any greatness in Euripides. In fact, Aristophanes sums up Euripides in a totally negative fashion:

> . . . this devil-may-care
> Child of deceit with his mountebank air (3, p. 994).

Murray observes that "[Aristophanes'] attacks are sometimes rough and vicious, sometimes acute and searching, [but] often enough they hide a secret admiration" (15, p. 13). Murray is not explicit about the secret admiration, but I suggest the following example as supportive of his statement: A character in *The Frogs* says to the character Euripides, "Tell me on what particular ground a poet should claim admiration?" The character Euripides responds, "If his art is true, and his counsel sound; and if he brings help to the nation, by making men better in some respect" (3, p. 971). This is a noble statement. It is followed by a rebuttal that is vacuous: Euripides does not make men better, he does the "reverse" and makes them "worse"; as a result, he deserves "the gallows" (3, p. 971). Why would Aristophanes make Euripides look so noble if he despised him? I conclude with Murray that Aristophanes does hide "a secret admiration" for Euripides. It does not seem so secret.

Aristotle's Summation of Euripides

From Aristotle's three major criticisms of Euripides—characters not elevated nor enhanced, choral odes irrelevant to context, and use of the god from the machine—one would expect that Aristotle would conclude that Euripides was an inferior playwright. But Aristotle surprises us. He concludes with a non sequitur: Despite his flaws, "Euripides . . . is . . . the most tragic of the poets" (4, p. 73). What elements of Euripides' writing override his flaws? Unfortunately, Aristotle fails to tell us.

Murray writes, Euripides is "capable still of thrilling his audiences with an intensity of tragic emotion such as no other poet had ever reached" (15, p. 15). Murray identifies the *intensity* of tragic emotion as the characteristic that makes Euripides "the most tragic of the poets" (15, p. 67). I suggest, in addition to intensity, that all those characteristics that make Euripides the most modern of the ancient Greek playwrights also serve to make him the most tragic.

WHY DID EURIPIDES WRITE *THE TROJAN WOMEN*?

A Response to Melos?

In the fall and winter of 416 B.C., a few months before *The Trojan Women* was produced, a terrible event occurred, which the Greek historian Thucydides recounted in great detail and at great length.

The small island of Melos had remained neutral during the Peloponnesian War and wished to remain so. This island had no military power. Athens sent envoys to Melos to persuade its council that the island should become subject to the Athenian empire. The envoys admitted that Melos had done nothing to offend Athens, and that Athens had no lawful claim to Melos. Athens simply did not wish any island to be neutral, believing that friendship with a neutral island implied that Athens was weak. If Melos would merely subjugate itself to Athens, nothing would happen to it; but if Melos chose to remain independent, Athens would have no choice but to destroy it.

The council of Melos responded that their only wish was to remain independent. The Athenians replied that this was not an option. The council responded that they chose to fight rather than accept slavery. The meeting was adjourned. The Athenians laid siege to Melos, captured it, massacred the men, enslaved the women and children, and occupied the city.

Several months later, in the spring of 415 B.C., Euripides produced *The Trojan Women*. Did Euripides write *The Trojan Women* in response to the attack on Melos? Was the play a protest, a political statement? The judges of the Athenian dramatic contest that season—who were, as usual, members of the political establishment—apparently saw no connection between Melos and *The Trojan Women*. They not only allowed Euripides to produce the play but also awarded him second prize in the competition.

Attributing the creation of *The Trojan Women* to Melos might suggest that Euripides was unaware of previous atrocities of this kind. What happened at Melos, however, was a typical Greek response to victory—and Euripides must have been familiar with the pattern. In 421 B.C., five years before the destruction of Melos, during the Peloponnesian War, the Athenians captured Scione, put all the men to death, and enslaved the women and children. Before Scione, when Platea surrendered to the Thebans in 427 B.C., its men were put to death, its women and children were sold as slaves, and the city was destroyed. And long before Platea, even before the carnage at Troy, Homer in the *Iliad* (Book 9, ll. 591–4) describes the typical experience of the vanquished: "[Here are] all the woes that come on men whose city is taken; the men are slain and the city is wasted by fire, and their children and . . . women are led captive" (11, p. 425).

To speak of Melos or Scione or Platea as the *reason* for Euripides' writing *The Trojan Women* is to minimize the play by particularizing it. Euripides was a great artist and was concerned with universal themes. As such, he probably wrote *The Trojan Women* not in response to

Melos, Scione, or Platea individually, but in response to all of them and to warfare in general.

Conclusion of the *Iliad*?
Homer's *Iliad* ends before the Trojan War is over. I have found this ending disappointing and unsatisfying. Perhaps Euripides had the same reaction. *The Trojan Women* provides the ending the *Iliad* lacks. Although many of the Greek playwrights wrote different versions of a particular story (for example, Aeschylus, Sophocles, and Euripides each wrote an *Oedipus* [5, p. 184]), only Euripides wrote a *Trojan Women* (8, p. 27). He clearly saw an original artistic opportunity that the other tragedians had not seen.

IMPACT OF THE TROJAN WAR UPON THE GREEKS
It is significant that the Greek poets and tragedians who sang of the fall of Troy sympathized not with the Greeks but with the Trojans. And no Greek writer evoked Greek guilt more than Euripides in *The Trojan Women*. However, Greek poetic literature dealing with the Trojan War must not be taken as a general expression of Greek political thinking. The Greeks' treatment of Melos demonstrates that. National self-examination, self-criticism, and self-condemnation were unique to the Trojan War. What was so different and special about the Trojan War to make the Greeks sympathetic to the Trojans?

The Trojan War was unique for several reasons. Unlike the war with Melos, the Trojan War was remote in time. It had taken place seven centuries before the golden age of Greece and the writing of *The Trojan Women*. This remoteness allowed the Greeks to view the war objectively and to see its immorality clearly: First, it was fought for a trivial reason, to bring back to Greece Helen, a self-indulgent woman. Next, even though the Greeks were victorious, the war resulted in great loss of Greek life. Furthermore, it resulted in the annihilation of Troy, a magnificent nation, which Homer repeatedly called "sacred" and whose people he described as "great souled." In the *Iliad* (Book 4, ll. 44–7), Zeus, "father of men and gods," speaks of Troy with these tender words: "For of all cities beneath sun and starry heaven wherein men that dwell upon the face of the earth have their abodes, of these sacred Ilios [Ilium] was most honoured of my heart, and Priam and the people of Priam" (11, p. 155). In the fifth century B.C., all Greece was acquainted with Homer's words. It is no wonder the Greeks felt guilt for the destruction of Troy.

Most significant in the Greeks' attitude toward the Trojan War, however, was a deeper psychological issue: the Greeks in the fifth century B.C. must have seen themselves as possible descendants of the Trojan women, who, when taken back to Greece as slaves, bore children fathered by their Greek oppressors.

In *The Trojan Women*, the Chorus Leader laments,

> This is the crown of war,
> this is the crown of sorrow,
> for women
> to bear the children
> of the enemy
> tomorrow!   (ll. 565–7, p. 94).

Although the Chorus Leader is weeping for the Trojan women raped at the moment of the destruction of Troy, the implication of her words for later generations of Greeks cannot go unnoticed. At least some members (and no Greek knew which ones) of the audience watching Euripides' play *were* "the children of the enemy tomorrow."

Furthermore, Hecuba's statement to Andromache that one day she may bear Greek children who will rebuild Troy (ll. 702–5, p. 106) was prophetic. Although the Greek descendants of the Trojan women did not rebuild a Troy of stone as Hecuba wished, they did rebuild a Troy of "everlasting themes," as she said they would (l. 1245, p. 155).

Therefore, the Greeks watching *The Trojan Women* must have had an ambivalent attitude toward their Greek ancestral fathers and, as a result, toward themselves. On the one hand they were proud of their ancestral fathers for their glorious victories; on the other hand they were ashamed of them because they knew that these same men had inflicted great pain on their Trojan ancestral mothers by destroying their families and homeland, enslaving them, and transporting them into exile in a foreign land— Greece.

Although the mixed Trojan ancestry of the Greeks must have had a stunning impact upon ancient Greek audiences and writers and must have been a major cause of Greek sympathy for Troy, sympathy is one thing and pride another. The Greeks were not proud of their Trojan ancestry, and they did not sing of it.

On the other hand, the people of another nation with Trojan ancestry—Italy—did show pride in their mixed Trojan ancestry. The difference in attitude between the Greeks and the Italians stems from the difference in sex, social status, and accomplishments of their ancestors: The Trojan ancestry of the Greeks came from Trojan women—slaves—who had nothing to do with the founding of the Greek nation. In contrast, the Trojan ancestry of the Italians came from Trojan men—heroes—who (unbeknownst to the Trojan women) escaped the massacre at Troy; these surviving Trojan men helped found the Italian nation. That was something the Italians could be proud of, and the Latin poet Vergil expressed that pride in his epic poem the *Aeneid*.

The Trojan heritage of the Greeks and the Italians enabled both peoples to look at the Trojan War as more than an event that happened to others. It happened to them. Although the Italians could and did sing proudly of their Trojan heritage, the Greeks could not and did not because that heritage was associated with profound shame.

Some say that the evidence that Troy existed or that a Trojan War ever took place is minimal. However true this may be, it would have no bearing on the ancient Greeks because they were confident that Troy once existed and that they were responsible for her destruction. The Trojan War impacted the Greek psyche like no other event real or imagined.

WAR

Although the evidence indicates that Euripides thought the Trojan War was immoral (that he wrote *The Trojan Women* provides sufficient evidence for that), there is no evidence that he was against war in general or that he was a pacifist, as has been asserted (10, p. 12).

On the contrary, Euripides recognized that there are times when a nation must fight. He never once has any character say that an invaded nation should not defend itself. But he does have a major character say that in the face of an aggressive or imperialistic enemy, a nation has the right to defend itself: in *The Trojan Women*, Cassandra says, "Our dead young men have had that greatest of glories—*They died defending their country!*" (ll. 386–7, p. 78). This is not pacifism. Cassandra also says that an invaded nation, should it win the war against its invader, has nothing to be ashamed of in victory. She warns, however, that any victory, even a justifiable one, is short-lived. On the other hand, a victory that is not justifiable is disgraceful.

Here is Cassandra's stand on war (three pithy lines in the original Greek):

> A thoughtful man shuns war.
> But if war comes to his nation,
> winning the victor's crown
> brings his nation no shame.
>
> However,
> even when the victor's crown
> is deserved,
> it is a perishable thing,
> and when undeserved,
> it is a disgrace! (ll. 400–2, pp. 79–80).

TROY, THE UNIVERSAL FALLEN CITY

In the twentieth and twenty-first centuries some adapters have tried to update *The Trojan Women* by substituting Hiroshima, Algeria, or Vietnam for Troy. Others have mistakenly assumed that *The Trojan Women*—perhaps because the word "women" is in the title—is a feminist play and adapted it with that preconceived notion in mind. These adaptations, designed to make the play more current and relevant, have degraded a universal work of art into a highly specific piece that, to paraphrase Barlow (8, p. 34), changes art into propaganda, which stirs the spectator for political rather than human reasons. Moreover, as these specific political pieces become less current and less relevant, the updated becomes the outdated.

However, the story of the fall of Troy never becomes outdated. Easterling has called it a "myth for all times" (5, p. 173). Therefore, the most modern setting for this most modern of ancient plays is and always will be Troy. That the fall of Troy happened over three thousand years ago does not diminish its powerful grip on us. Watching *The Trojan Women* is at times almost unbearable because of its relentless portrayal of human suffering and the gods' indifference to this suffering. Moreover, while the play portrays the annihilation of Troy and of the Trojan people (the men through battle and massacre, the woman and children through exile, slavery, and assimilation), it suggests the possibility of a similar annihilation of any nation at any time. It may even suggest the annihilation of civilization itself because of mankind's readiness to respond to emotion with violence rather than with reason.

Scholars, for example Barlow (8, p. 32), consider Hecuba to be the protagonist of *The Trojan Women* because she is the central figure. She gives the play its cohesiveness and articulates most clearly the theme of hope, survival, and endurance in a play otherwise filled with death, destruction, and despair. Hecuba's very first word and the first word of the play is "Up!" (l. 98, p. 55). Near the middle of the play Hecuba observes, "Death means nothing.   Life means hope" (ll. 632–3, p. 100). And Hecuba's final words, after all is lost and Troy itself is an inferno going up in smoke, are "forward into the new day of slavery!" (l. 1330, p. 163).

Although Hecuba is the conventional protagonist, I suggest there may be a different protagonist in the play, one even more cohesive and central, more important and tragic than Hecuba. That protagonist is Troy itself. Troy is the consummate and most nurturing Trojan woman. It is Troy that Hecuba mourns, as do all the Trojan women, in ever-growing intensity from the beginning of the play to the end. The Chorus laments:

> Sing, O Muse,
> a song of Troy.
> Sing with tears
> in a strange new tune
> music for the grave.
> I sing an ode for Ilium—
> how she died,
> unhappy slave! (ll. 511–15, p. 90).

While other cities have become symbols of the ravages of war (Jerusalem, Coventry, Dresden, and Hiroshima, to name a few), no city has symbolized it more universally for the Western world than Troy. Euripides' use of a nation as the protagonist of a play would have been something new in tragedy.

THIS ADAPTATION

In making my adaptation, my principal concern was to convey to the modern audience Euripides' ideas as clearly as he expressed them to his audience. Therefore, just as Euripides used ordinary Greek speech to convey his ideas, I used ordinary English.

My second concern was whether to make changes responsive to those criticisms of Aristophanes and Aristotle that I considered valid—the defective prologue, the irrelevant choral odes, and the *deus ex machina*. I decided to make the changes because I thought to do so would best serve a modern audience. Therefore, my translation is an "adaptation"—not in the sense of a current or updated version of the play but in the sense of a revision in response to ancient criticism that in my judgment remains valid to this day. As a result, I have made the following changes:

I have rewritten the Prologue with material that gives the background of the play. This replaces Euripides' prologue, which does not provide information that a modern audience requires.

I deleted the gods Poseidon and Athena from the Prologue because these gods are distracting, and their message about a punitive storm is irrelevant. Whether they are walk-on characters or gods from the machine is moot.

I have reworked the choral odes based in large part on Euripides' material but organized to give meaning and purpose to the dialogue, to augment the themes under discussion, and to help a modern audience better understand the play. An exception is the ode on the Ruse of the Trojan Horse, which I left essentially intact, because this ode, apart from being beautiful and dramatic, is relevant to its context in the play.

I deleted the mythology in the choral odes concerning the earlier destruction of Troy (at the hands of Hercules and Telamon) because such mythology is esoteric as well as irrelevant, and thereby particularly confusing to a modern audience. I omitted allusions to Ganymede and Tithonus for the same reasons, but I did not discard the imagery concerning them when it was wonderful. I simply rewove it into the context. I deleted most of the long synopsis of the *Odyssey* delivered by Cassandra because it is tedious and irrelevant. On the other hand, I slightly augmented some allusions or descriptions where Euripides was thin because I wished to clarify his ideas or make them more meaningful to a modern audience.

I made other changes as well, not mentioned by Aristophanes or Aristotle:

I divided the play into two acts, with an intermission at the place where there is a sharp dramatic break in speeches and action. There is no evidence that all ancient Greek plays were performed without interruption, and reason as well as artistry suggests that at the original performance there was a break here. Members of a modern audience need a break to catch their breath, perhaps wipe away a tear, and share feelings of sadness with others before facing the last half of the play. There is no reason to believe that ancient audiences did not have the same needs.

Euripides' stage directions are lost. A play without stage directions is difficult to perform or follow. Therefore, with the help of director Barry Bosworth (see Acknowledgments), I have provided stage directions that were tested and were effective in the Granite Hills Acting Workshop's production of this adaptation.

I do not recommend the use of Greek theatrical or full masks in performing *The Trojan Women*. In ancient Greece, masks enabled male actors to play female roles, and different masks allowed one actor to play several roles. These reasons do not apply to a modern production. Some have suggested that Greek theatrical masks also permitted the actors to project their voices, but there is no evidence to support that. The contrary seems more likely; full masks seem to muffle voices. Full masks have the added disadvantage of disguising who is speaking.

On the other hand, I do suggest the use of domino or half masks. They were effective in the Granite Hills Acting Workshop's production. Dominoes do not muffle voices nor prevent the audience from determining who is speaking. In addition, actors who played Greeks wore masks, and those who played Trojans did not, which readily enabled a modern audience to discriminate between Greeks and Trojans. Masks, even dominoes, which are plain, are somewhat frightening. Using dominoes for the Greeks thus helps to dramatize the enemy's partially faceless and frightening inhumanity. Finally, a mask for Helen reminds the audience that "Helen of Troy" is in fact a Greek, and also permits the actress who plays the role to become "the most beautiful woman in the world."

Now that I have explained what I have done and why I have done it, on with the show!

THE TROJAN WOMEN

CHARACTERS

HECUBA—a slave, only recently queen of Troy;
        widow of Priam;
        mother of CASSANDRA, Paris, and Hector;
        mother-in-law of ANDROMACHE and HELEN;
        grandmother of ASTYANAX
TALTHYBIUS—herald of the Greek army
CASSANDRA—a slave, only recently a princess of Troy;
        daughter of HECUBA;
        oracle of Apollo
ANDROMACHE—a slave, only recently a princess of Troy;
        daughter-in-law of HECUBA;
        widow of Hector;
        mother of ASTYANAX
ASTYANAX—a slave-child, only recently a prince of Troy;
        grandson of HECUBA;
        young son of ANDROMACHE and Hector
MENELAUS—a Greek king and general;
        husband of HELEN;
        brother of Agamemnon
HELEN—a Greek queen, wife of MENELAUS;
        widow of Paris;
        daughter-in-law of HECUBA

CHORUS LEADER—a slave, a Trojan woman of middle age
CHORUS OF TROJAN WOMEN—slaves (nine to eleven in number), mostly young
SOLDIERS of the Greek army (four to six in number)

SCENE: *A prisoner-of-war camp on the Trojan plain just outside the city walls. The entire Trojan plain was recently a battlefield.*

TIME: *Early morning, one or two days after the end of the Trojan War, during the thirteenth or twelfth century B.C.* (When Euripides wrote this play, in the fifth century B.C., the Trojan War was already ancient history or mythology.)

SET: *Sea and sky upstage.*
   A large stone block encircled at random by clumps of wildflowers stands near downstage center.
   A portion of the walls of Troy are stage left. The walls are made of gigantic stone blocks that ascend from floor to stage ceiling and in the mind's eye beyond. (In a Greek theater, the tops of the walls are visible and may be twenty-five feet high or higher.) The walls are in two staggered segments angled slightly toward upstage center. The upstage segment is recessed several feet behind the downstage segment and angles and extends more than the downstage segment toward upstage center.
   The gap between the segments represents the entrance to the city, not visible to the audience. This design creates the illusion that the city gates are wide enough to admit the great Trojan Horse, which is alluded to but not seen in the play. In reality, and for the purposes of the play, the gap need be only wide enough to admit a two-wheeled cart large enough to transport an adult, a small child, and some Trojan booty.
   A ruin is upstage center and right, beyond which are the sea and sky. The ruin is a pile of small to medium-sized stone blocks from a Trojan tower, recently fallen from the top of the city walls. The blocks are artfully arranged to create the illusion of randomness, but in fact the stones form a stack of five concentric semicircular platforms resembling half of a five-terraced hill. (These directions apply to a customary Roman theater. A large Roman theater or a Greek theater, however, could accomo-

date the entire "hill" of the ruin.)   The foot of the ruin makes an irregular arc facing downstage and the city walls.   Functionally the ruin serves as a low staircase on which much of the action, including some of the choral dancing, takes place.   The most upstage steps, which are located beyond the crest of the ruin, are not visible because they are blocked by the crest, but they are necessary for entrances from and exits to the direction of the sea.

Three pavilions (henceforth called simply tents) stand stage right, all in downstage-upstage alignment but slightly angled so that the most upstage is most center stage.   Only the downstage tent, most extreme stage right, rests on the floor of the stage (or, in a Greek theater, in the orchestra).   The other two tents are located on the ruin.   The upstage tent rests near the crest of the ruin; and the middle tent rests in between the upstage and downstage ones.

There are three approaches to, or exits from, the stage or orchestra: (1) to or from Troy: stage left, through the entrance to the city, already described; (2) to or from the harbor: stage right, downstage of the tents; and (3) to or from the sea: upstage right, over the crest of the ruin.

MASKS: *The Greeks wear domino masks (soldiers wear masks beneath their helmets).   The Trojans do not wear masks.*

WIGS AND HELMETS: *The Trojans and Greeks wear long, flowing and curly brunet wigs except Menelaus, whose wig (and beard) is blond, and Hecuba, whose wig is gray, closely cropped, and unevenly shorn. Talthybius and Menelaus' wigs are tied by fillets.   The ordinary Greek soldiers do not wear wigs under their helmets.   Talthybius does not wear a helmet but carries one, at least through Act One.*

PROLOGUE

The sea and sky are pale gray (and remain so almost to the end of the play).

After a moment, an actor who will shortly play the Greek herald, TALTHYBIUS, *enters downstage right from the direction of the harbor. He is partially costumed in a Greek soldier's tunic and corselet; he carries his helmet— which he does not don or wear during the Prologue or play—greaves, sandals, wig, and mask. His clothing and skin are clean (as are those of all the characters who play Greeks).*

Soon after, an actress who will shortly play the CHORUS LEADER, *a Trojan woman, enters stage left from the city entrance. She is wearing a full-length gown characteristic of Trojan women. She is also wearing a black shawl. Her gown is shabby, somewhat dirty and tattered, even ragged, and it is rent at the neck, but its former elegance is still apparent. She is carrying a wig and sandals. (The women of the* CHORUS, *skin patchily dirty and wigs somewhat disheveled, wear similar costumes but do not wear shawls.)*

Stage lighting comes up.

The two PROLOGUE ACTORS *begin speaking to the audience. They will have completely donned their costumes, and the* CHORUS LEADER *will have also smudged her face, arms, and gown, before the Prologue ends when both actors will have entered character.*

1–97[1]

> Actor/TALTHYBIUS: Ladies and gentlemen,
> I play Talthybius, the Greek herald . . .

> Actor/CHORUS LEADER: . . . and I play
> the Chorus Leader
> in the play you are about to see,
> *The Trojan Women* by Euripides.

Actor/TALTHYBIUS: The Trojan War has just ended.
    It was a war
    between the Trojans and the Greeks,
    fought here on Trojan soil—
    a brutal and costly war
    that lasted ten long years,
    with great carnage on both sides.

    It was fought for a trifling reason:
    Helen, the most beautiful woman
    in the world
    and wife of King Menelaus of the Greeks,
    ran off to Troy with Paris,
    a prince of Troy.

    Menelaus' brother, King Agamemnon,
    raised a great army to win Helen back.
    Well, now the war is over,
    and we Greeks have won it.

Actor/CHORUS LEADER: (*pointing upstage*)
    We are standing
    just outside the walled city.
    You see before you
    a portion
    of the famous plain of Troy,
    where many battles were fought.
    Now it is a desert
    (*pointing*) with only a patch of wildflowers
    here and there.
    Once great trees stood here,
    groves sacred to the gods.

    (*pointing stage left*)
    Those are the walls of Troy—
    high walls that encircle the city,
    great walls with towers—
    walls built by the gods

Apollo and Poseidon,
who once loved Troy
above all cities.

There (*pointing to the ruin*)
is a ruin—a fallen tower.
Yesterday the Greeks,
with the help of the gods,
knocked the tower down,
even though our walls and towers
were "indestructible."

And there
(*pointing somewhat upstage left*)
is one of the entrances to the city.
The gates themselves are gone, burnt.
The city is smoldering.

The goddess Athena
sent within these walls
a horse pregnant with armed men,
a horse that brought this devastation
you see before you now.

Future generations will remember
this great wooden horse
and they will call it "the Trojan Horse"—
this horse built by Greeks—
because it brought about
the fall of Troy.

Actor/TALTHYBIUS: The Trojan Horse
       will live forever
       in history.

Actor/CHORUS LEADER: The shrines of the gods
       are desolate
       and running with blood.
       On the steps of the altar

to Zeus the Protector,
the Trojan king, Priam, lies dead,
killed by a Greek soldier.

The Greek victors
carry great heaps of gold—
Trojan loot—
down to their ships.

Actor/TALTHYBIUS: (*pointing stage right*)
Over there is the harbor
where the Greek ships are at anchor.
Now we Greeks
are preparing to return home.
We are waiting for a fair wind
to take us to the joyful sight
of wife and children,
family and friends—
loved ones not seen for ten years.

Actor/CHORUS LEADER: The devastation
has left the Trojan temples empty.
The gods have gone away.
And all our Trojan men
have been killed
by Greek spears.

All the Trojan women—
mothers, wives, daughters, and sisters
of the dead men—
and all the children
are now prisoners of war.

Actor/TALTHYBIUS: Down by the river Scamander,
not far from here,
you can hear echoes of weeping,
cries from women assigned to soldiers
in a lottery.

(*pointing upstage to the tents*)
You see before you
a special prisoner-of-war camp.
In these tents are Trojan women
not assigned by chance.
They were handpicked
by the Greek generals themselves.

In one of the tents
is a Greek woman, Helen,
the cause of the war.
I have nothing more to say about her.

(HECUBA, *in character, startled and frightened, oblivious to the* PROLOGUE ACTORS, *suddenly wanders out of the most downstage tent. The* PROLOGUE ACTORS *watch her. She is dressed like the other* TROJAN WOMEN. *Using a walking stick,* HECUBA *walks just beyond stage center, looks at the Trojan gate, and shakes her head. Then, facing downstage center, she slowly lies down, curling on her side and shutting her eyes.*)

Actor/CHORUS LEADER: If there is anyone
who deserves your pity,
for she knows misery like none other,
(*pointing to* HECUBA)
look at the old woman lying over there
near the entrance to the city.
That is Hecuba.
She was queen of Troy, Priam's wife.
She weeps many tears
for many dead.

Gone is Hecuba's husband,
the great king Priam.
Gone, too, are all her glorious sons,
among them the mighty Hector,
commander in chief of the Trojans,

all dead.

Actor/TALTHYBIUS: One grief
          is still hidden from her:
          At this very moment,
          her daughter Polyxena
          is being murdered—
          Polyxena, promised as a gift to Achilles,
          the great Greek warrior.

          Achilles was killed
          just before the fighting ended.
          Paris, Helen's lover,
          shot an arrow that struck Achilles
          in the one place he was vulnerable,
          his heel.
          Achilles died and was buried.

          But we Greeks
          have kept our word to him.
          We have given him
          the promised Polyxena.
          A Greek soldier has just slit her throat
          over Achilles' grave.

Actor/CHORUS LEADER: That leaves Hecuba
          only one child,
          one daughter,
          Cassandra, wild and mad,
          Cassandra, the virgin
          who—people say—
          always prophesies the truth
          but never is believed.

Actor/TALTHYBIUS: King Agamemnon,
          commander in chief of the Greeks,
          has selected Cassandra
          for his very own.

(*donning his wig, then holding up his mask*)
All Greeks in this play wear masks
to indicate the face of the aggressor—
strange, inhuman, frightening.
It is the face of the foreigner and invader
in this land.
(*donning his mask*)

Actor/CHORUS LEADER: (*turning to face the walls*)
Look!
This is Troy! This is Ilium!
A city and a nation happy once,
famous and magnificent!
Soon all will be ashes!

Actor/TALTHYBIUS: Men are fools to lay waste
a city and a nation,
and bring desolation to her temples,
her graves, and her holy places.

Actor/CHORUS LEADER: The gods bring destruction
to men like these!

(TALTHYBIUS *exits downstage right in the direction of the harbor; the* CHORUS LEADER *enters a tent.*)

(*Darkness descends.*)

ACT ONE

HECUBA *is lying on the ground in the same position as at the end of the Prologue. She opens her eyes and stares for a moment.*

HECUBA : (*to herself*) Up! Wretched old woman!
 Lift up your head from the ground!
 This is no longer Troy,
100 and you are no longer her queen.
 Your fortune has changed.
 Bear it and survive!

 (*With the help of the walking stick, she slowly pulls herself up to a semi-sitting position and faces the audience.*)
 The winds of fate are like the winds at sea.
 The wind picks up, the wind dies down.
 Sail with the wind! Sail with the tide!
 Sail before the breath of God
 on the ship of life!
 Turning the bow into the wind
 is futile.
 Let the ship go as it will
 on the winds of fortune.

 (*With the help of the walking stick, she slowly stands, massages her low back, then walks over to and sits down on the stone block near downstage center.*)

Sorrow upon sorrow!
What sorrow is not mine?
My nation, my husband,
and my children
are gone.
The wealth and glory of my ancestors
are gone.
In the end, everything came to nothing.
And I witnessed it all.

There is nothing I cannot tell you.
And yet, what good would it do?
Why sing a song of grief?

How unhappy I am!
Cruel destiny has forced me
to lie down here.
(*striking the ground with her stick*)

(*rubbing her temples, then her neck, then
the sides of her chest*)
Oh, my aching head, neck, chest!
Oh, my aching body!

(*again striking the ground with her stick*)
This bed is very hard,
and my body is racked with pain.
It might help to move around a bit,
to rock my body from side to side
(*rocking*) and move it
to the tune of endless tears.

(HECUBA *walks to stage center, stops, and
begins to sob uncontrollably; after a moment, she composes herself.*)
Sobbing is the music of grief.
It brings relief to weeping hearts.

120

(*Suddenly entranced, she hums a simple
martial tune, then angrily strikes the stick
upon the ground in rhythm to the tune.*
HECUBA *continues to tap the stick while
speaking*:)
Greek ships chanting a war song
sung to tuneful flutes and pipes
sailed with swift oars
across the dark blue sea
from the fair harbors of Greece
to holy Troy.
The music they made was joyful to them
but hateful to us.
(*stopping the tapping*)

O Greeks!
When you found our harbors,
you dropped your anchors
held with well-made line,
cables of Egyptian flax.
You dropped grief
into Trojan waters.

(*to the audience*)
What were they looking for?
What made them come?
A woman! Helen! Hated by all!
The wife of Menelaus,
shame to husband and to home!
Because of her,
Priam, the king, my husband,
father of fifty boys,[2] was slain.
And now she has shipwrecked me!

(*moving to the stone block
and sitting on it*)
I am the queen—
Hecuba!
And oh, how I suffer—

run aground upon a reef,
shattered, and destroyed!

What a place this is
where now I sit in dust,
here in the prisoner-of-war camp
of Agamemnon,
the mighty Greek king!

140   I, an old woman,
am being led
far away from home,
a slave
with shorn head,
bruised and bowed,
in mourning for my dead
without number
and our past glory.

(HECUBA *turns and stares at the walls of
Troy. Then she stands and walks toward
stage center and calls to the* CHORUS *in the
tents*:)
Troy is smoldering.
Let us weep for her,
O Trojan women full of sorrow,
wretched wives of warriors
who carried spears of bronze.

Like a mother bird crying over her young,
I shall lead the weeping.

(*suddenly reflecting on happy days, eyes
closed, smiling*)
Oh, once I sang a different tune
and praised the Trojan gods,
and we danced so joyfully,

(*cheerfully tapping her foot rhythmically,
then turning through 360 degrees, arms
and stick held high*)
with rhythmically beating footsteps,

(*facing the audience, then turning her
head to one side as if someone dear were
beside her*)
while Priam watched,
leaning on his scepter,

(*turning to heaven*)
and the gods, too, listened to the music,
and watched the dancing,
and smiled.
(*lost in happy memory*)

(*Half the members of the* CHORUS *of* TROJAN WOMEN
*emerge from the tents in single file, slowly walking
toward* HECUBA. *They assume various stations on
the ruin and stage and stand motionless like columns. They wear costumes similar to those of the*
CHORUS LEADER *and* HECUBA.

*Their movements are meaningful, appropriate
to the context of the spoken lines. Although here
the members of the* CHORUS *are formal and static,
elsewhere they dance singly or in groups, coming
together or dispersing, grouping and regrouping,
gesturing, or pantomiming. When they are motionless, they stand like columns or sit like statues,
often in relaxed postures. Only a few specific
stage directions are provided.*

*As for their speech, most of the time they speak
individually or in groups of two or three, reciting
only one stanza; then another member of the*
CHORUS *speaks the next stanza; and so on in a
chain. Separate stanzas are indicated by extra
space between lines. From time to time, the*
CHORUS *members speak in unison for a single*

stanza, but at the onset of the subsequent stanza, they revert to speaking as individuals—although there are no stage directions, apart from these, to indicate that.)

CHORUS LEADER: Hecuba,
      why are you talking to yourself?

CHORUS: And why so loudly?

      What is it you are saying?

      What were you saying before?

      I could hear your pitiful grieving
      even in my tent.

      (*in unison*)
      Fear stabs the hearts
      of Trojan women
      sorrowing
      over their slavery.

HECUBA: (*turning and pointing to the harbor*)
      O children,
      look there! It's begun!
      Greek oarsmen on their ships
160   are beginning to row.

CHORUS LEADER: (*running to the top of the ruin, looking toward the sea*)
      O ships,
      where are you taking me?

CHORUS: (*looking toward the harbor*)
      Has the time come
      to carry me over the sea?

      —to a strange country far from home?

HECUBA: I don't know any more than you do.
>One thing I know:
>when hope is gone,
>fear remains.

CHORUS LEADER: (*speaking to the* CHORUS *members
>still inside the tents*)
>Awake, unhappy Trojan women!
>Come out of your tents
>and learn of the slavery that awaits you.

>The enemy is preparing
>for the voyage back to Greece.
>The first ship—
>I can see the flashing oar blades!—
>has just begun to sail!

HECUBA: (*to the* WOMEN)
>Hush!
>Do not awaken Cassandra!
>It's best for her to stay in her tent
>while she's delirious and insane.
>To see the Greeks mock her madness
>would wound me even more.

>O Troy, Troy,
>suffering as you die!
>Those who leave you—
>the living and the dead—
>are suffering, too.

(*The remaining* CHORUS *members emerge from
their tents, walking toward* HECUBA *slowly in single
file.*)

CHORUS: Trembling in fear,
>I leave the tents of the Greek king
>Agamemnon

to listen to you, my queen,
and learn my fate.

Are the Greeks going to kill me
here and now
and end my misery?

(*facing the harbor*)
Or will their sailors—
I can see them on the sterns!—
take me to their ships
now that they prepare to sail?

HECUBA: (*facing the last* WOMAN *to speak, then
turning to the audience*)
Oh, my child,
in the early hours of morning,
I was suddenly terrified.
Panic-stricken,
my heart wildly beating,
I awoke and left my tent.
It was dawn.

CHORUS LEADER: (*to* HECUBA)
Has the Greek herald come?
Whose slave am I to be,
poor creature that I am?

HECUBA: (*to the* CHORUS LEADER)
You will learn your assignment
soon enough.

CHORUS LEADER: Which Greek will take me where?

CHORUS: To the Greek mainland?

Or to an island in the middle of the sea?

HECUBA: Ah, me! Ah, me!

Whose slave shall *I* be?
Where shall I live out my life as a slave,
an old woman,
gray, dried up, and frail—
utterly worthless!—
a living corpse,
a shadow of my former self,
a ghost hovering over a dead man's grave?

Will I be a doorman for my master
or a nursemaid to his children,
I, who once was
(*sitting*) queen of Troy?

CHORUS LEADER: Poor woman!
          How will the tears
          you shed now
          compare with the degradation
          yet to come?

200   CHORUS: No longer shall the shuttle fly
          to and fro on Trojan looms.

          No more will I see
          my parents' house.

          (*in unison*)
          No more!

CHORUS LEADER: I see a worse fate still:
          a Greek
          carrying me
          to his bed
          in the dark.

CHORUS: (*in unison*)
          Curse such a night
          and such a fate!

I see myself a slave in Corinth
forced to draw water
from its famous spring.

(*enthusiastically*)
If I had a choice,
I would go to Athens,
the great and happy city.
I hope I go there!

(*sullenly*)
I hope I don't go to Sparta,
to the palace of despised Helen,
by the treacherous and turbulent waters
of the river Eurotas,
where as a slave,
I would have to face Menelaus,
ravager of Troy.

(*enthusiastically*)
I've heard that the hallowed land
at the foot of Mount Olympus
drinks from an ever-flowing river
and is beautiful and fertile,
with flowering trees and vineyards.

(*enthusiastically*)
That would be my second choice,
after Athens, the holy city!

(*enthusiastically*)
Sicily! I want to go there!
The land of Mount Etna,
the erupting volcano,
mother of Sicilian mountains,
and home of the God of Fire.

Sicily is far across the sea
opposite the land of the Phoenicians.

220

It is famous for young men's games
and their laurel wreaths of victory!

I've heard about them, too,
and the mountainous land
near the Ionian Sea
where from on high
you look down
on waves falling on beaches.

There, too, the waters
of a beautiful and sacred river
(*pausing, smiling, and stroking her hair*)
turn brunettes to blondes—
or redheads—

and bless the land
with young men
who are handsome
and brave
and true!

CHORUS LEADER: (*anxiously; pointing to the harbor;* ALL *turn.*)
          Here comes the herald
          walking swiftly
          from the Greek camp!

CHORUS: He brings bad news,
          without a doubt.

          What news now?

          What is he going to tell us
          we don't already know?

          (*in unison*)
          What more do we need to hear?
          We already know

we are slaves to the Greeks!

(TALTHYBIUS *enters rapidly downstage right, from the direction of the harbor, with two* SOLDIERS *behind him, and walks up to* HECUBA, *who rises to her feet to face him. The* CHORUS *recoils in fear.*

The SOLDIERS *are fully armed with spears, swords, and helmets. One* SOLDIER *stations himself at the top of the ruin and faces the audience, spear shaft held in right hand, right arm fully extended laterally and horizontally, shaft butt against outside of right foot, shield held in left hand against chest.*

The other SOLDIER *stations himself by the downstage tent and faces the walls of Troy, spear shaft held vertically in right hand, slightly in front of him, elbow flexed, shield held in left hand against chest.*)

TALTHYBIUS: Hecuba!
            I feel I can call you by your name
            because we are old friends.
            Many times I came across the plain
            from the Greek camp to Troy.
            You remember me.
            I am the Greek herald,
            Talthybius.
            (*He places a hand on* HECUBA'*s shoulder; she recoils, turning her back on him.*)
            I bring you news.

HECUBA: (*facing and walking toward the* CHORUS)
            Just what we've been dreading,
            dear Trojan women!

TALTHYBIUS: (*to the* CHORUS)
240   I have all your assignments,
            if that is your fear.

HECUBA: (*facing* TALTHYBIUS*; harshly*)
       Where are we going?
       —to a city in Thessaly?
       —to the city of Thebes?

TALTHYBIUS: You have been assigned individually,
       each to a different king,
       not as a group.

(*The* CHORUS *members become agitated.*)

HECUBA: Who gets whom?
       Can any Trojan woman expect happiness?

TALTHYBIUS: I know the answers.
       But ask your questions one at a time,
       not all at once!

HECUBA: First, my stricken child Cassandra.
       Tell me,
       to which king does she go?

TALTHYBIUS: To Agamemnon!
       He chose her over all the others
       as his *special prize*.

HECUBA: To serve his Spartan wife?
       How sad that makes me!

TALTHYBIUS: No! No! Not her!
       To serve the king himself
       at night
       in his own bed
       as his bride.

HECUBA: No! Never!
       Cassandra belongs to a god!
       She is a virgin,
       sacred to golden-haired Apollo!

He gave her the gift
of life without marriage!

TALTHYBIUS: Agamemnon
is madly in love with her.

HECUBA: (*thinking out loud*)
Cassandra, my child,
throw away
your holy crown of laurel leaves
and your sacred necklace of flowers!

TALTHYBIUS: (*wryly*) Well, now,
a king's bed is not so bad.
(*walking amidst and staring at the women;
selecting one, gently stroking her cheek*)
Many would consider themselves lucky
to be brought there.

260   HECUBA: And what of my youngest child,
whom you took from me
early this morning?
Where is she?

TALTHYBIUS: (*pretending ignorance*)
Do you mean Polyxena?
Or another child?

HECUBA: (*angrily*) Polyxena!
To whom is she assigned?

TALTHYBIUS: Hers is a privileged assignment.
She attends Achilles' grave.

HECUBA: I bore a daughter
to attend a grave?
What are you saying?
Is that a Greek custom?
What a strange ritual,

(*mockingly*) *old friend*!

TALTHYBIUS: Consider your daughter lucky.
            She is very well off indeed.

HECUBA: What do you mean?
         Why do you speak like that?
         Is she alive?

TALTHYBIUS: Her work is not hard,
            and she is fulfilling her destiny.

HECUBA: (*not quite understanding, changing the
         subject, while each woman of the* CHORUS
         sorrowfully bows her head)
         And what of Andromache,
         wife of my son Hector,
         splendid soldier,
         what is in store for her?

TALTHYBIUS: Achilles' son, Pyrrhus,
            chose her as his prize
            from all the others.

HECUBA: And whom am I to serve,
         with my shaking head and weak limbs,
         I who need a walking stick
         to keep from falling?

TALTHYBIUS: You are the slave
            of the King of Ithaca,
            Ulysses!

HECUBA: (*beating her head and clawing at her
         cheeks*)
         Oh! Oh! I beat this shorn head
         and claw these cheeks
         and cry in despair!

280

It is my lot
to serve that hateful liar,
that evil man of treachery,
that enemy of justice,
lawless monster!
With forked tongue and double-talk,
he twists everything
from one end to the other and back again,
turning even his friends into enemies.

(*to the* CHORUS)
Weep for me, Trojan women,
for my bad luck.
I am ruined, lost.
I, poor soul, have fallen on the worst lot,
and my bitterest days are yet to come.

CHORUS LEADER: (*to* HECUBA)
At least you know your fate, O Queen!
But what about me?
Which Greek master is mine?

TALTHYBIUS: (*ignoring her; to his* SOLDIERS)
Men,
go and bring Cassandra out here at once
so that I may deliver her
to Agamemnon,
the commander in chief
of all the Greek forces!
(*to the* CHORUS LEADER)
After that I shall give the others
their assignments.

(*A bright, flickering light flares up and
jumps about in the middle tent.* ALL *momentarily freeze.*)

Look there!
What is the meaning

of this burst of flame?
Is it a torch?
Are Trojan women
setting fire to their tents
300   because they are about to be taken
to Greece?
What is going on here?
Are they setting themselves on fire,
choosing death over sailing with us?

(*aside*)
How cruel is the yoke of slavery
when placed on the necks
of those who so recently
enjoyed freedom!

Untie the tent flaps!
Open them up!

(*The* SOLDIERS *run to the lighted tent.*)

Death may bring joy to Trojan slaves,
but not to their Greek masters,
and least of all to me,
for I shall be blamed!

HECUBA: (*to* TALTHYBIUS)
No! No!
Nothing is being set on fire!
No one is burning a tent!
It is my daughter Cassandra,
driven mad
by the sweet breath of a god.

(CASSANDRA *emerges from the lighted tent holding
high a torch. She is wearing a dirty and ragged
full-length white gown, a crown of laurel leaves,
and a floral necklace.*)

CASSANDRA: I hold it up!
           I show it!
           I carry the torch!

           See how I revere this temple!
           I make it ablaze with light!

           (*singing and dancing*)
           O God of the Wedding Celebration!
           Begin the dance!
           Begin the song!

           Blessed am I, the bride,
           and blessed is he, the groom!
           For in a royal wedding at Argos,
           I marry a king!

           O God of the Wedding Celebration!

           (*to* HECUBA)
           Mother, stop weeping and wailing
           over my father's death
           and grieving over our beloved country!
           This is a wedding celebration
           and I am getting married!

           It is customary
           on such an occasion
320   to make the torch
           as bright and radiant
           as the stars and the moon
           to honor
           the God of the Wedding Celebration
           and the Goddess of Night.

           Everyone, prepare to dance!
           (*dancing*)
           Dance! Fly, feet, fly!
           Just as we did in happy times

while my father was still alive.
Divine is the dance!

(*drawing a circle around herself in the air
with the torch*)
Lead the dance,
O Apollo,
here in your temple!
(*love-stricken, pretending to dance with
the god*)
I, crowned with laurel,
make a sacrifice to you.

(*dancing and laughing madly*)
Dance, Mother! Laugh, Mother!
Just as I laugh!
Join in the dance!
(*taking* HECUBA *by the hand and encour-
aging her to dance*)
Come dance with me!
Follow my lead—
a step here, a step there!

(HECUBA *reluctantly takes a step or two
with* CASSANDRA, *then stumbles and falls
while* CASSANDRA *continues dancing bizar-
rely.*)

Sing the wedding song!
Celebrate the bride
and her happiness and joy!

O God of the Wedding Celebration!

(*turning to the* CHORUS *dressed in rags*)
Come, beautifully dressed women of Troy!

(*The* CHORUS *members look on in embar-
rassment and horror.* HECUBA *stands.*)

Sing to the groom,
who destiny has decreed
340   shall lie by my side
in my bed!
(*continuing to dance in a wild and bizarre
way, while humming, and intermittently
hugging and trying to kiss members of the*
CHORUS *or* TALTHYBIUS *and the* SOLDIERS,
*whose necks, cheeks, chests, or thighs she
occasionally strokes*)

CHORUS LEADER: (*embarrassed, turning to* HECUBA)
My queen,
Will you not stop your daughter
in her madness,
before she runs to the Greek camp
doing this?

HECUBA: O God of Fire,
You bear torches at happy weddings!
But the torch you bear
that is burning here—
dancing this way and that,
so savage, so wild—
is one of pain.

It is not as I wished!

O Cassandra,
I had such high hopes for you!
O my child,
I never dreamed
you'd enter a marriage
where on your wedding night
a Greek spear
would force itself upon you!

Give me the torch!

It sheds no holy light!
You are not even carrying it straight!
You move about so wildly.
Your fate has not restored you
to your senses.
You are mad as ever.

(CASSANDRA *continues to dance and hum.*)

Take the torch, women of Troy.
Let us exchange her wedding song
for our never-ending tears.

(CASSANDRA *thrusts the torch at individual women
of the* CHORUS, *who cringe in fright, until one of
them snatches it and extinguishes it.* CASSANDRA,
*looking like a wounded child, stops dancing
abruptly and sucks her fingers dejectedly.*)

CASSANDRA: (*suddenly, to* HECUBA *in mock jubila-
tion*) Mother,
crown my head with triumphal wreaths
and be happy!
For I marry a king!

Escort me to my lord,
and if I seem the least bit hesitant,
(*grimly emphatic*)
send me to him by force!

Mother,
I tell you,
as the god Apollo lives,
(*menacingly*) Agamemnon,
renowned lord of the Greeks,
in marrying me
will make a deadlier marriage
than Helen ever did.

I will see to it
that Agamemnon is murdered,
and I will make his house
as desolate as he has made ours,

360   and avenge my brothers' blood
and my father's, too,
in my triumph!

(HECUBA *turns away in despair*.)

(*aside, coolly, intimately*)
I shall not tell of other things
my marriage shall bring—
the ax that one day soon
shall fall on my neck,
and other necks, too,
nor of the boy
who will murder his own mother,
nor of the bringing down
of the House of Atreus!
(*laughing madly*)

(*to* HECUBA, *who turns to face her*)
Now I shall prove to you
that this nation of ours
(*looking at the city walls*)
is more blessed than that of the Greeks.
I know I am mad.
But in this matter,
I am perfectly sane:

(*pointing to* HELEN's *tent at the crest of the
ruin; all eyes turn there*)
For the sake
of one woman
and one act of love,
the Greeks hunted Helen down,
and, in so doing,
killed thousands.

Agamemnon, their commander in chief,
considered so wise a ruler,
what did he do in his wisdom?

He killed the child he loved
for the sake of the woman he hated:
he sacrificed his daughter Iphigenia,
who delighted him so,
the loveliest daughter
any father could want,
to avenge his brother Menelaus
for Helen,
who had run off willingly.
It's not as if she was taken to Troy
by force.

And when the Greeks came to Troy
(*circling* TALTHYBIUS *and each* SOLDIER,
*looking at them and touching them seduc-
tively*), they died,
one after another.

(*looking* TALTHYBIUS *straight in the eye*)
What for?
It's not as if Greece were invaded
and the Greeks robbed
of their land.

All the Greeks
whom the God of War
transported to Troy to die
never saw their children again.
And their bodies
were not wrapped in shrouds
by the soft and gentle hands
of wives and loved ones.
Instead they lie buried
in angry and alien soil.

Back home in Greece,
things were no better.
Many women
died widows, many childless!
And aged parents waited for sons
who never appeared again,
well-raised boys—
all in vain!—
never to tend
parental graves.
So much for Greek glory
and victory!
(*laughing madly, facing* TALTHYBIUS)

As for the Trojans,
our dead young men
have had that greatest of glories—
They died defending their country!

When Trojan blood filled the plain,
when fierce Trojan men were killed—
silenced by the spear—
they were carried home by loved ones,
their dead bodies wrapped in shrouds
and buried
in the loving and embracing earth
of their native land.

And those Trojan men
who lived to fight another day
spent those days
not lonesome in a foreign land.
After a hard day's battle,
they returned home
to the company of wives and children,
pleasures denied the Greeks.
(*looking and laughing at* TALTHYBIUS *and
the* SOLDIERS)

As for Hector,
whose fate seems so cruel to you,
listen to me!
I speak the truth!
He may be dead and gone,
but of all men he is the most famous.
He died the hero of heroes,
and all men sing his glory
and of his true and brave heart.

Troy's invasion by the Greeks
is the cause of Hector's fame.
Had the Greeks stayed at home,
who would have known
how wonderful he was?
Before the Greeks invaded Troy,
who even heard of Hector?

Listen to me!
Had the Greeks stayed home,
who would have heard of Paris,
my brother
(*to* HECUBA) and your son?

Paris married Helen,
the daughter of a god,
of Zeus no less!
Had Paris not married her,
he would have married
a more ordinary girl
whom no one
would ever have known
or talked about.

(*declaratively and directly to the audience*)
A thoughtful man shuns war.
But if war comes to his nation,

winning the victor's crown
brings his nation no shame.

However,
even when the victor's crown
is deserved,
it is a perishable thing,
and when undeserved,
(*directly to* TALTHYBIUS) it is a disgrace!

(*to* HECUBA) For these reasons, Mother,
weep no more for our country or its dead,
and weep no more for my marriage!

For by this union,
I shall destroy those
whom we hate most!
(*laughing*)

CHORUS LEADER: (*to* CASSANDRA, *who suddenly sits
down on the ground, giggling, sucking her
fingers, and humming*)
You laugh at your own misfortunes,
and you sing of things best left unsung.

TALTHYBIUS: (*to* CASSANDRA)
You are crazy!
Had Apollo not made you mad,
you would have to pay the price
for speaking so badly of our generals.
We are about to sail from this country,
and your words are a bad omen.

(*aside*)
Those who are great
and wise by reputation
are no better off
than those who count for nothing.

Agamemnon,
most powerful king in Greece,
beloved son of Atreus,
loved by all his countrymen,
is chained by a passionate love
of his own choosing.

(*contemptuously walking up and down,
scowling at* CASSANDRA; *abruptly stopping,
puzzled, to the audience*)
He loves this mad woman
above all women,
whereas I, an ordinary man,
never once even wanted
to go to bed with her.

(*to* CASSANDRA, *who rocks and mumbles*)
You! Your mind is not quite right.
So, as for your denunciation of the Greeks
and praise of the Trojans,
I never heard one word of it!
Your words
are like leaves carried on the wind.
Your lips do not understand
the words they speak.

420

Now, follow me to the ships,
you who are the *perfect* match
for our general!

(*to* HECUBA)
And you, Hecuba,
when Ulysses sends for you,
go to him at once!
His wife, Penelope,
whose slave you will be,
is a good and gentle and wise woman,
so men say.

CASSANDRA: (*crawling to downstage center, aside*)
He is pompous,
this messenger boy!

Oh, heralds, heralds!
Why do you have such an honorable name
when you are hated by all?
You walk with your head in a cloud—
above it all!—
unconcerned that you bring bad news
of dark anguish, often of death.
And so you are universally despised,
the tools of tyrants and mighty nations.

(*standing, walking, and speaking to*
TALTHYBIUS)
You say
my mother will go to Ulysses' palace.
That's not what Apollo told me!
He said she would die right here in Troy!

(*ashamed of her disclosure*)
But why should I upset her
by speaking of such things?

Ulysses, horrible man!
Little does he know
of the troubles that await him!
All our troubles and all of Troy's
will seem like gold compared to his.
Ten years behind him spent here,
ten years before him yet,
and to cut the story short,
he will come home
with no survivors on his ship
440   except himself,
and find countless troubles
in his house
when he finally gets there.

But why should I speak of *his* troubles,
why prophesy about Ulysses
when I have no intention
of forewarning him?
Let us get on
to *relevant* matters—
my forthcoming marriage
in the house of death!

Agamemnon, great king of the Greeks,
you think that Fortune has smiled on you
and that you have won all!

Well, the dust that skims the earth
has a higher bed than you!
Base man that you are,
so shall you die!
You shall be buried dishonorably,
not by light of day,
but under cover of night,
you, the leader of the Greeks,
who thinks you have accomplished here
something really wonderful!

As for me, on our wedding night,
they will cast me, naked and dead,
into a ravine.
And after wild animals have fed on me,
storm floods raging with winter rain
shall deliver me, Apollo's servant,
to you, my groom, in our burial bed!

(*caressing her floral necklace*)
Good-bye, garlands of the god Apollo,
God of Prophecy,
with whom I'm still so much in love!
Good-bye, wondrous necklace
that honors him!

The festivals I once delighted in
I celebrate no more.

(*A breeze comes up.* CASSANDRA *strips off
her necklace of flowers.*)
I tear you from my neck
while my body is still untouched
and while I still wear white,
and give you to the winds
to carry away.

(*scattering the flowers on the wind*)
Go!

(*turning to* TALTHYBIUS, *matter of factly*)
Where is the general's ship?
Where am I to board?

(*prophesying*)
Agamemnon, be sure to catch
the first morning breeze
to fill your sails! (*laughing*)
You take a Fury along
when you take me from this land!

(*turning to* HECUBA)
The time has come
to say good-bye, Mother.

(HECUBA, *weeping, embraces* CASSANDRA
and covers her with kisses. The two
SOLDIERS *forcibly pull* CASSANDRA *away
from* HECUBA, *one* SOLDIER *on either side,
each restraining* CASSANDRA *by an arm as
she struggles to get free. They hold her
fast; she ceases struggling, whereupon
they relax their grip;* CASSANDRA *speaks to*
HECUBA:)

Mother, do not weep.

(*facing the city walls*)
O country that I love,
good-bye!

(*breaking free of the* SOLDIERS *and falling
to the ground*)
O dear brothers and dear father,
lying beneath the earth,
good-bye!
Soon I shall be with you.

(*The* SOLDIERS *lift* CASSANDRA *and hold her
fast as they slowly drag her, facing* HECUBA
and the CHORUS, *in the direction of the
harbor.* CASSANDRA *shouts*:)
460   I shall come in triumph
to the land of the dead
after I ruin the House of Atreus,
which has ruined us all!
(*laughing madly*)

(TALTHYBIUS *and his* SOLDIERS *lead* CASSANDRA,
*laughing, offstage right, in the direction of the
harbor, all eyes upon them. When they are out of
sight, the breeze dies down, and* HECUBA *falls first
to her knees, then flat on the ground.*)

CHORUS LEADER: (*to two members of the* CHORUS)
You! Attendants of Hecuba,
don't you see that your mistress,
an old woman,
has fallen to the ground?
Help her!
How can you let
an old woman lie there?
Women!
Lift her up!

(*The two* WOMEN *stoop to lift* HECUBA.)

HECUBA: (*waving them off*)
No! Leave me alone!
Let me lie where I have fallen!

(*The two* WOMEN *back off.*)

Kind acts unwanted are not kind at all.

Trojan women,
are you surprised I cannot stand
when my burden is so heavy?
Anguish now, anguish before,
and anguish still to come!

(*head slowly turning and arms slowly
reaching to heaven*)
O gods!

(*lowering head and arms, then facing the
audience*)
But why call on them?
When do they help?

(*reflecting*)
And yet,
there's something within all of us
that cries out to God
when trouble comes.

(*slowly standing*)
I shall sing one last time
of our happy days of old,
hoping that the contrast
between now and then
will inspire some pity in the gods.
Then I shall resume

my song of woe.

I was from a royal family.
I married into a royal house.
I had royal children,
many sons I bore my king,
not mere nothings,
but fine, brave boys, the very best,
princes, lords of Troy.

Such sons!
No other Trojan woman—
or Greek—
(*sweeping her arm over the audience*)
or stranger in the whole wide world
had sons like mine!
I was so proud of them!

But I saw them fall, all of them,
one by one,
beneath Greek spears.
And I cut off my hair
lock by lock
and laid each lock in mourning
at each son's desolate grave.

And after Troy was captured,
I wept for Priam, their father.
I did not hear of his death from others
but saw it with my very own eyes—
these same eyes that weep for him now—
when the Greeks butchered him
at our household altar
to Zeus,
Our Protector!

I raised my daughters
to marry well—
to marry brave men and kings—

and I fully expected them
to leave my house one day.

But I did not expect them
to marry *Greeks*!
Now they are gone, all of them,
and I have no hope
of ever seeing them again!

(*walking about agitatedly*)
Finally,
to crown my absolute misery,
I am going to Greece
in my old age
to be a slave!

The tasks they give women of my age
are the most menial of all.
I shall have to stand at the door,
always ready to open or shut it
for my *master* and his family.

I, who bore Hector,
shall grind meal for baking bread,
and at the end of the day,
lay this decrepit old body,
which once slept in a royal bed,
down upon the ground,
torn rags covering torn flesh.
(*angrily, weeping*)
It is humiliating for royalty
(*pointing to her clothing*)
to wear garments like these.

Oh, the pain
already inflicted on me,
and the pain
that is yet to come,
all because of the self-indulgent love

of one woman!

(*throwing herself down upon the ground*)
Cassandra, my child,
pure of heart and pure of soul
and inspired by a god!
Soon a Greek man's hands
will remove your sacred clothing,
fondle your sacred body,
and take away your virginity.

And you, sweet Polyxena,
where are you?

I had so many children,
but now,
not one son or daughter
can help me
in all my pain.

(*Two members of the* CHORUS *stoop to lift*
HECUBA *up; she waves them off.*)

Why raise me from the ground?
What good will that do?
Once on my feet, where will they lead me,
feet that came so majestically to Troy
and now are so enslaved?
Will they lead me to a bed of straw
and a stone pillow
where I may cast this body down
and drown it in a sea of wasted tears?

To think
that once
I was considered fortunate!
Never call anyone "fortunate"—
until he's dead!

CHORUS LEADER: Sing, O Muse,
            a song of Troy.

            Sing with tears
            in a strange new tune
            music for the grave.

CHORUS: I sing an ode for Ilium—
            how she died,
            unhappy slave!

            A great four-wheeled platform
            carried a giant wooden horse
            to the city gates.

            The Greeks left it there.

            (*in unison*)
            This horse
            enslaved us all.

CHORUS LEADER: (*pantomiming*)
            It was a beautiful thing,
            a towering steed
520   trimmed with gold on the outside—
            but inside hiding iron,
            deadly Greek spears,
            quiet then,
            but soon rattling so loud
            heaven could hear.

            For you see, within the horse,
            Greeks were hiding.

CHORUS: From the stone towers and walls,
            the Trojan people cheered:

            (*in unison*)
            "The war is over!"

"The wooden horse
is a gift to Athena,
great Trojan goddess,
daughter of Zeus!"

"Bring the holy statue
into the city!"

CHORUS LEADER: And the horse was pulled
                over the threshold
                and through the city gates.

CHORUS: What young girl then,
              what old person,
              did not run from home
              to watch, with song and rejoicing,
              young Trojan men
              hauling the horse
              into the city?

          All the people of Troy
          rushed from their homes
          in excitement
          to see it.

          (*in unison*)
          All Troy fell in love
          with Death in disguise.

CHORUS LEADER: This thing,
              so beautifully carved
              from mountain pine
              and polished to a radiant gloss,
              this gift to the virgin Athena,
              who loved horses
              and kept an immortal team of steeds
              for her chariot,
              was waiting to take Troy by surprise

and kill her.

(*The members of the* CHORUS *pantomime as
the* CHORUS LEADER *continues speaking*:)
The Trojans,
with much straining and groaning,
like men drawing the hull
of a great ship to land,
pulled the wooden horse
with giant cables made of spun flax,
through the high and wide gates
of the city.

They drew it
to Athena's temple,
even its floor paved with marble.

540   CHORUS: (*in unison*)
It brought Death
to our country!

CHORUS LEADER: And when evening fell,
all that exertion
to set the horse in its holy place
filled everyone
with exhilaration.

CHORUS: Everywhere
torches were ablaze!

And when the music started—
the pipes and the flutes—
young girls danced
and sang joyous songs.

CHORUS LEADER: Every Trojan home
was radiant with light
through that splendid night
when no one slept.

Finally, just before dawn,
Fatigue sent the city to sleep.

(*The members of the* CHORUS *pantomime
falling asleep except one* WOMAN *who
dances.*)

Within Trojan homes,
the torches burning low
continued to give off
a dark and flickering glow,
casting light on faces
still content
even after sleep set in.

As for me,
I was still singing and dancing
in honor of the virgin Athena,
daughter of Zeus.

Suddenly,
a bloodcurdling cry rang out!

(*A member of the* CHORUS *delivers such a cry. The
rest of the* CHORUS *pantomimes awakening terrified.*)

CHORUS: It ran through the city,

up the broad streets,

down the narrow alleys,

possessing in its tight grip

(*in unison*)
the entire Trojan nation!

Terrified children
clutched at their mothers' dresses
with trembling hands.

CHORUS LEADER: For the Greeks
            lurking in the horse
            had come out!

560   CHORUS: (*in unison*)
            The God of Slaughter
            had come forth
            from his hiding place . . .

CHORUS LEADER: . . . to carry out Athena's plan!

At the altar to the goddess,
many Trojans already lay *sacrificed*,
their blood still running.

And while newly married young men
lay in deep sleep in their beds,
Greeks hacked off their heads.

Blood flowed everywhere,
and in the frightening dark,
people stumbled on headless things.

(*declaratively*)
And the wives of those men
got a *little prize*!

(*walking downstage center, to the audience, slowly*)
This is the crown of war,
this is the crown of sorrow,
for women
to bear the children
of the enemy
tomorrow!

CHORUS: (*all heads bowed*)
> O weep, Trojan women,
> weep for Troy!

CHORUS LEADER: (*pointing stage left to the city gate*)
> Hecuba! Look! (ALL *look*.)
> It's Andromache
> in a cart
> pulled by an enemy soldier!
> She is holding
> close to her heaving and sobbing breast
> her young child,
> dearest Astyanax,
> Hector's sweet son.

(HECUBA *slowly rises and turns to face the cart pulled by a Greek* SOLDIER. *Sitting within the cart is* ANDROMACHE, *holding* ASTYANAX. *The cart is piled high with Trojan treasure, including golden urns, Hector's bronze spearhead, and his large round bronze shield; the cart railing is draped with a beautiful red Trojan fabric. The cart comes to a halt stage center, just upstage of* HECUBA. *The* SOLDIER *stands at attention by the cart during the following scene.*)

CHORUS LEADER: (*to* ANDROMACHE)
> Where are they taking you in a cart,
> most forlorn of women,
> with the bronze weapons of Hector
> and Trojan spoils
> captured by Greek spears?

CHORUS: What Greek temples will be adorned
> by these treasures taken from Troy?
>
> Or do these trophies go

to mountain shrines in Thessaly?

ANDROMACHE: (*sardonically*)
        I go where my Greek master takes me.

(ANDROMACHE *and* ASTYANAX *descend and walk hand-in-hand to* HECUBA, *who embraces them.*)

HECUBA: Sorrow upon sorrow!

ANDROMACHE: You are singing *my* song!

(HECUBA *sits down upon the block;* ANDROMACHE *sits down beside her;* ASTYANAX *kneels against the block downstage, one hand on his grandmother, the other on his mother.*)

HECUBA: Woe! Woe!

ANDROMACHE: Oh, the pain! Oh, the pain!

HECUBA: O Zeus!

580   ANDROMACHE: Zeus cares for our pain?

HECUBA: (*calling*) Children!

ANDROMACHE: Once! No more!

HECUBA: Troy is gone,
        and all her treasure!

ANDROMACHE: Anguish!

HECUBA: And my children,
        my well-born children,
        are gone!

ANDROMACHE: Woe! Woe!

HECUBA: Mine! All mine!

ANDROMACHE: Misfortunes
>   for our city, our nation . . .

HECUBA: . . . in its shroud of smoke!

ANDROMACHE: (*standing, searching, then calling
>   out*)
>   Come back to me,
>   Hector, my husband!

HECUBA: O Andromache!
>   My son, to whom you cry,
>   is in the grave.

ANDROMACHE: Defend your wife,
>   abused by the Greeks!

HECUBA: Hector,
>   my first child, whom I bore to Priam,
>   is dead!

ANDROMACHE: Lead me to death!
>   I cannot bear life without you!

HECUBA: We all bear troubles!
>   We all suffer!

ANDROMACHE: My lost city!

HECUBA: More pain added to heavy pain!

ANDROMACHE: (*to* HECUBA)
>   The gods warned you
>   that Paris would bring
>   about our destruction.
>   You should have killed him

at his birth,
as the gods commanded.
But instead you let him live.

Now the gods have thrown down
the towers of Ilium
because of his love for
that accursed woman.

Blood-covered corpses
lie at the feet of the goddess Athena,
food for vultures.

600   Paris made Troy a slave!

HECUBA: Oh, desolate country!

ANDROMACHE: I weep for you, O Ilium,
          as you are being forsaken!

HECUBA: How is this going to end?

ANDROMACHE: O home
          where I gave birth to my son!

HECUBA: Children,
          your mother has lost a nation,
          and she has lost you, too!
          I shed tears upon tears!

          The living must grieve
          and go on living.
          Death alone
          brings an end
          to tears and pain.

CHORUS LEADER: Tears are somehow sweet,
          and the words and music of grief
          are soothing to the soul.

ANDROMACHE: Mother of Hector,
hero whose spear
killed so many Greeks
on this very battlefield,
look out on it now!

HECUBA: I see the handiwork of the gods!
First they build something
(*pointing and scanning from the bottom to
the top of the city walls*)
that reaches the sky.
That impresses men
but amounts to nothing.
Then the gods knock it down
to drive home their point.

ANDROMACHE: My child and I
are being taken away
as spoils,
royalty reduced to slavery,
great change of circumstance.

HECUBA: The power of fate is terrifying.
Only a moment ago
Cassandra was forcibly torn from me.

ANDROMACHE: There is still something
for which you must suffer.

620   HECUBA: There is no end to my sufferings.
No counting them.
Evil upon evil.

ANDROMACHE: Your daughter Polyxena lies dead.
Her throat was cut over Achilles' grave,
a gift to him in death,
a corpse for a corpse.

HECUBA: Oh, such cruelty!
That is what the herald Talthybius meant
when he spoke in riddles.
I could not understand
because it was much too clear.

ANDROMACHE: I just saw her myself
and got down from the cart
to cover her body with my cloak
and beat my breast.

HECUBA: Polyxena, my child—murdered!
What an evil sacrifice!
How viciously you were slain!

ANDROMACHE: She is dead,
but happier by far
than I who live.

HECUBA: O my child,
life is not the same as death!
Death means nothing.
Life means hope.

ANDROMACHE: Death is no different
from never having been born.
And death is better by far
than a life of pain.

After experiencing the pain of life,
the dead one no longer suffers.

When someone
who has known real happiness
loses it
and goes on living,
640   that person is a lost soul.

Polyxena is dead.

That is the same
as if she'd never been born.
Now she knows nothing
of her past suffering.

As for me,
I aimed for a good reputation—
and achieved it!
But when I aimed for good fortune,
I missed the target completely!

(*stage center*)
I tried to be a perfect wife,
and look at my reward!
I did all the things
wives are supposed to do
to win men's praise.

Even virtuous women
are criticized
if they do not stay at home.

So I set aside my yearning
to go outside,
and stayed home.
And I never let small talk
or gossip in.
My own thoughts
were enough for me.
I was resourceful
and had in myself
and in my home
the soundest of teachers.
I craved nothing more.

Each day
I welcomed Hector home with a smile.
I listened to his troubles
and soothed him with a calm demeanor.

I knew when it was right
to have my own way
and when it was right
to yield to his wishes.

And wouldn't you know it!
Report of my behavior
reached the Greek camp
and was my undoing!
For as soon as I was captured,
Achilles' son, Pyrrhus,
wanted me for his wife!

660   Now I shall be a slave
to men who murdered my husband!

O Hector! O dearest!

If I thrust aside the memory
of my darling Hector's face,
and open my heart to the man
who now will come to my bed,
am I not a traitor to the dead?

But if I withdraw my body
from my new husband,
will he not hate me?

They say
one night in a man's bed
is all it takes
to win a woman over.

And yet,
I cannot but wonder at the woman
whose lips forget her first husband
and with fresh kisses loves another.

Not even a horse,
when separated from its mate,
will easily bear the yoke
with a new one.
And yet
we call such animals dumb,
lacking reason,
and lower in nature than man!

My dearest Hector,
in you I had everything in abundance
that I wanted in a husband—
love, understanding,
rank, wealth, courage.

You took me from my father's home
before I'd ever felt a man's touch.
And on our wedding night
you yoked me,
a young virgin,
fast to you,
and made me yours forever.

Now you are dead.
I shall be taken with other plunder
in a Greek ship,
yoked in slavery.

(*to* HECUBA)
680   Mother, is not Polyxena's death
less worthy of your weeping
than my suffering?
For me there does not even exist
that last refuge of every person—
Hope.
I shall not lie to my heart—
however sweet such dreams may be—
that things may still turn out
all right for me.

CHORUS LEADER: We share your pain,
        Andromache.

CHORUS: (*in unison*)
        In lamenting your own ruin,
        you teach us the depths of our own.

HECUBA: (*taking* ASTYANAX *by the hand and
        walking to stage center with him, then
        kneeling down before him, and pointing
        downstage right to the harbor, encourag-
        ingly*)

        Look, over there, at the ships!

        (*He looks in that direction, then turns back
        to face her.*)

        You know,
        I myself have never been aboard a ship,
        but I know what happens on them
        from pictures I've seen
        and things I've heard.

        If a storm comes,
        but the wind is moderate,
        the crew is happy
        even though the work is hard.
        One sailor mans the helm,
        another tends the sails,
        still another bails.

        But if the sea is heavy
        and the winds are strong,
        then the sailors must yield to fate,
        surrender to the wild waves
        and the lashing rain,
        broken men, without control,

leaving all to chance
and hoping for the best.

And that is how it is with me
right now.

(*turning and standing, talking to* ALL, *but
continuing to hold* ASTYANAX *by the hand*)
I have so many troubles
there is no one word
that describes them all.
No good will come of cursing,
no good to wish for a different fate.
Let things be.

So powerful is the storm,
so mountainous are the waves
the gods have sent on me,
that I am drowning—
sinking into the deep—
no longer here.

(*to* ANDROMACHE)
But Andromache, dear child,
you must stop mourning for Hector.
Your tears cannot bring him back.

Honor your new lord.
Give your new husband a reason
700   to love you for your sweet ways.
Use them and allure him.

If you do this,
you will please all your loved ones,
and you may bring up my grandson
(*smiling down at* ASTYANAX)
among his enemies
to help Troy in the best possible way.

Rear this boy, my own boy's child,
to manhood.
Remember, too,
you may have other children in Greece,
who may one day rebuild Troy.
Imagine!
Troy once more a great city!

(ALL *notice* TALTHYBIUS *and his two*
SOLDIERS *approaching from the direction
of the harbor.* ASTYANAX *becomes frightened and runs to* ANDROMACHE *and clings
to her.* HECUBA *continues*:)

Ah!
I see a new matter
that will take us far away from this one.

Who is this coming?
The herald of the Greeks?
Again?   So soon?
What news this time?

TALTHYBIUS: (*entering and stopping;   to* AN-
DROMACHE)
Andromache, wife of Hector,
who was the bravest heart in Troy,
do not hate me.
Against my will I come to tell you
words from the Greek leaders.
They were unanimous.

ANDROMACHE: What are you trying to say?
You are hinting
that you are about to give us
more bad news.

TALTHYBIUS: It has been resolved . . .
(*hesitantly, pointing to* ASTYANAX)

that your son here . . .
How can I say this?

ANDROMACHE: Surely not that he and I
are to travel on different ships?
—not that he and I
are to have different masters?

TALTHYBIUS: No! (*shaking his head and pausing*)
No Greek shall ever rule this boy.

ANDROMACHE: Is he to be left behind, then,
all by himself,
all alone in Troy,
the last survivor of the Trojan people?

TALTHYBIUS: I do not know an easy way
to tell you such bad news.

ANDROMACHE: I appreciate your concern.
But unless the news is unbearably bad . . .

TALTHYBIUS: (*swiftly, loudly, clearly*)
Your son must die!

(ALL *freeze*.)

(*turning away*)
There! I've said it!
Now you know the hard truth!

(ALL *unfreeze*.)

ANDROMACHE: (*wailing*) Ah, me!
(*falling to her knees, hugging* ASTYANAX;
to TALTHYBIUS)
The news you bring
720   is far worse than anything
I have ever seen or heard.

TALTHYBIUS: (*defensively*) It was Ulysses!
    He spoke to all the assembled Greeks,
    and his motion carried.

ANDROMACHE: Aiee! Aiee!
    This is pain beyond all measure!

TALTHYBIUS: Ulysses persuaded them
    that the son of a hero
    must not be allowed to live.

ANDROMACHE: (*angrily*) May his words
    fall on his own sons!

TALTHYBIUS: He said . . .
    the child . . . must be flung . . .
    from the walls of Troy.

    (ANDROMACHE *slowly stands. She lifts*
    ASTYANAX *and presses him against her
    breast. Then, like a trapped animal, she
    darts here and there, running toward sev-
    eral* TROJAN WOMEN, *who look on help-
    lessly. Looking at* HECUBA *in despair, she
    sets* ASTYANAX *back down upon the
    ground. Then she falls to her knees and
    hugs him tightly, while looking despair-
    ingly at* TALTHYBIUS.)

    (*walking toward* ANDROMACHE; *kindly*)
    Just let it be done
    and you will show great wisdom.
    Do not cling so hard to the boy.
    Suffer as a brave woman
    with unbearably bitter pain,
    as befits you.

    But do not think you are strong

when you have no strength at all.
You are powerless.

Woman, look at the circumstances!
Look around!
(*scanning the* CHORUS)
Do you see anyone who can help you?

There is no one to help you!

(*scanning the walls of Troy, the ruin, the tents*)
Do you see any sanctuary for refuge?

(*decrescendo, pausing after each statement*)
Your nation has fallen!
Your husband is dead!
You are a prisoner!
You are a slave!
You are alone!

One woman
and *all* of us!
How can you battle against us?

(*intimately*) For your own good,
stop struggling.
This will bring you no shame.
No one can ridicule you for submitting.

(ANDROMACHE *is about to speak.* TALTHYBIUS *holds out his hand to her face.*)

And please! I beg of you!
Do not curse the Greeks or their ships!
For if you say anything
to make the army angry,

this son of yours will not be buried,
and no pity will be shown you.
Silence is best.

Bear your sorrow as well as you can
and your dead child will be buried,
and you will find the Greeks
more inclined to kindliness.

(*Despairing and terrified,* ANDROMACHE *kneels before* ASTYANAX. *She strokes his head and cheeks
and combs his hair with her fingers.   Then, wiping
away her tears, she talks to him calmly.*   ASTYANAX
stares into her eyes.)

740   ANDROMACHE: O my darling,
               dearest child,
               too much honored!
               You will die
               at your enemies' cruel hands
               and leave your mother forlorn,
               never to be consoled.

               Your father's nobility
               has not turned out to your advantage.
               He could save others,
               but he cannot save you.

               (*turning to the* CHORUS, *then to the audi-
               ence*)
               O my wedding and marriage bed!
               All has turned to misery!

               I was so happy
               when long ago I came
               to my husband's palace,
               to Hector's house.
               I did not think I would bear a son
               to be a sacrificial victim for Greeks,

but to be a king
of a great and fertile nation.

(ASTYANAX *clutches* ANDROMACHE; *her
gaze returns to him.*)

Are you weeping, my little one?
Do you see the terrible fate
that awaits you?

(ASTYANAX *tries to hide under her arms.*)

Why are you clutching
and clinging to my dress,
little bird, trying to nestle under my wings?

Your father, Hector, will not come.
He will not return from the grave.
He will not burst forth from the earth,
his famous spear in hand, to save you.
Nor will any of his brothers, your uncles,
nor any of those
who made up the Trojan might.

(*hugging* ASTYANAX)
What will it be like,
plunging (*slowly, emphatically*)
down, down, down—
oh, horrible!
Your neck will be broken in a deadly fall
from a great height,
and your life's breath will be snuffed out
with no one to pity you.

(*gazing into his eyes*)
O my darling child—
oh, how I love you!—
such a little thing,
so dear to your mother's heart!

(*drawing him close*)
Oh, the sweet scent of your skin!

(*stroking him*)
How I loved to nurse you!
Was it all for nothing
to hold you to my breast
when you were wearing diapers?

760

Was it all in vain
that I gave birth to you
and wore myself out with labor pains?

And all my caring—
when I ran after you
when you rushed headlong into danger,
and when I watched over you
all through the long nights
when you were sick,
till I grew weary with watching.
All that wasted?

Come now,
kiss your mother one more time,
one last time,
then never again.
Lean against my breast.
Embrace me.
Throw your arms around my neck,
and press your lips to mine
(ASTYANAX *responds accordingly.*)

(*Slowly standing,* ASTYANAX *clutching her,*
ANDROMACHE *turns to* TALTHYBIUS *and the*
SOLDIERS; *angrily*)
O Greeks—*civilized* Greeks—
who devise atrocities and tortures
outstripping the barbarian nations!

Why are you killing my son,
who did you no wrong—
an innocent child
in no way responsible
for all the terrible troubles we bear,
both Greek and Trojan alike?

(*holding* ASTYANAX *by the hand, walking
up to and confronting* TALTHYBIUS; *pointing to the tent most upstage*)
It is Helen you want,
not my son!
Helen, the daughter of Tyndareus,
a mere mortal man,
not the daughter of a god,
not the daughter of Zeus!

Oh, she has many fathers!
Vengeance! Jealousy! Murder! Death!
All the plagues of the earth!
Those are her fathers,
not Zeus!

It is Helen who is responsible
for this plague on countless Greeks
and Trojans alike!
It is Helen who ought to die!

Helen with her beautiful eyes
brought ugly death
to the famous plains of Troy!

(*defiantly and desperately*)
It is Helen you want,
not my poor child!

(TALTHYBIUS, *in a sign to his* SOLDIERS,
snaps his fingers and nods. One SOLDIER
pulls ASTYANAX *away from* ANDROMACHE

by the arm. The other SOLDIER, *the one
who towed the cart, now forces* AN-
DROMACHE *toward the cart as she continues to speak*:)

Go ahead!
Carry him away!
Fling him! Fling him
to his death,
if that is your wish!
(*angrily and loudly and in giant sobs*)
Feast on his flesh!

(ANDROMACHE *is shoved into the cart.*)
The gods are destroying me,
and I cannot lift one finger
to save my child.

(*from the cart*)
Oh, cover my poor body
and fling me headlong onto a ship!
This is a fine marriage I am entering
where the family of the groom
is preparing
to slay my child!

(ANDROMACHE *covers her head and shoulders with
the red fabric in the cart, and reaches out weeping
to* ASTYANAX, *who in turn reaches out to her as the
cart is towed off downstage in the direction of the
harbor. After the cart is out of view, the* CHORUS
LEADER *speaks.*)

780   CHORUS LEADER: Unhappy Troy,
you have lost tens of thousands
for the sake of one woman
and her hateful marriage.

TALTHYBIUS: (*taking* ASTYANAX *by the hand away from the* SOLDIER *to downstage right; kneeling in front of him, placing his hands on* ASTYANAX's *shoulders and looking him straight in the eye*)
Come, my boy,
now that you have left
the loving embrace
of your poor mother . . .

(*pointing and looking up at the top of the walls;* ASTYANAX *also looking*)
to the topmost top
of the ancestral walls with you,
where it has been decreed
your life shall end.

(*nodding to a* SOLDIER *who walks to* ASTYANAX; *standing and turning his back to* ASTYANAX *and facing the audience; to the* SOLDIER)
Take him!

(*The* SOLDIER *takes* ASTYANAX *by the hand and faces the walls but does not move.*)

(*to the audience*)
The herald who delivers such news
has to be a man who feels no pity
and enjoys cruelty.
I am not the right man for the job.
(*walking off downstage, in the direction of the harbor*)

(*The* SOLDIER *now walks rapidly with* ASTYANAX *toward the city gates. Just before arriving there,* ASTYANAX *breaks free of the* SOLDIER's *grasp and runs to* HECUBA, *who all the while has been watching him from downstage center.*)

HECUBA: (*kneeling and embracing* ASTYANAX)
O child, child of my own unhappy child,
whose toil was all in vain.
Your mother and I
are being unjustly robbed of your life.
Your life is our life, too! *Ours!*

(*The* SOLDIER *pulls* ASTYANAX *away from*
HECUBA *toward the city gates, while*
ASTYANAX *struggles to run back to*
HECUBA.)

(*watching*) What will become of me?
What can I do for you, so ill-fated?
I can beat my head and breast like this.
(*alternately beating her head, then her
breast with both fists*)
Over this at least I still have control.

(*The* SOLDIER *comes to a stop before entering the city gates and slowly raises his
head to scan the top of the walls.*
ASTYANAX *stops struggling, turns to face
the walls, and also looks upward. The*
CHORUS, *having withdrawn toward the
tents, watches in horror. The* SOLDIER *and*
ASTYANAX *walk slowly through the gates.*)

(HECUBA, *standing erect, turns to the audience; the* CHORUS *looks at* HECUBA *in anguish.*)
My nation is gone!
And my grandson
will soon be gone, too—
the last of the royal family!

Is there anything remaining for us?
Is there anything we have not suffered?

And now,
(*speaking ever more slowly*)
we are to be annihilated
in an instant.

(*She stares at the audience as the lighting slowly fades.*)

INTERMISSION

ACT TWO

Hardly any time has elapsed between Acts One and Two.

The CHORUS *dances, alternately idyllic in remembrance of former days and sorrowful in mourning for the present.* HECUBA, *watching, is sitting on the block.*

799-859[3]

CHORUS LEADER: Waves break
on Trojan beaches,
our home overlooking the sea.

Once happy women
danced and sang here
in front of a glorious city
loved by the gods.

CHORUS: Once we had olive groves,
gray-green leaves flashing in the sun,

and orchards, boughs laden with fruit,

and we could hear
the buzzing of bees.

But the gods did not remain.
They abandoned us
without pity.

Ilium is laid waste,
hated by the gods.

(*in unison*)
The Greek spear
has destroyed
the land of Priam.

CHORUS LEADER: The gods made the Greeks
a sea-faring people
who sailed the wide waters.

CHORUS: They came over the sea
to the harbor of the river Simois,
where they anchored
and beached their boats.

From there they could see
the high walls of Troy,
walls that the gods
Apollo and Poseidon built
stone upon gigantic stone.

These walls
were *indestructible*!

CHORUS LEADER: The gods drink wine
poured from golden jars
into golden bowls,
wine that brings them joy.

CHORUS: Divine lips drain divine cups,
while our city burns
and her plain lies wasted.

The sea groans, the coast moans,
and the lonely beaches mourn
husbands and sons,
aged parents, revered ancestors,
and dead heroes.

The rivers and coves

where we used to swim
and the fields where we used to play
are desolate.

Where are the riders
who loved to ride horses
bareback on beaches?
Now only pebbles roll to and fro,
covered with foam.

No more shall a Trojan prince,
with his youthful charm
and his twinkling eyes
so sincere and reverent,
serve the altar of Zeus.

(*in unison*)
The Greek spear
has destroyed
the land of Priam.

CHORUS LEADER: And the lovers,
          where are they?

CHORUS: The first love that came to these shores
          was the love of the gods themselves.
          The gods built the city walls
          and lifted them high into the sky,
          and then joined themselves in marriage
          with Ilium.

          (*in unison*)
          How exalted then she was!

          Now the gods stand and watch
          as Ilium is dying.

          Even the white-winged Dawn,
          once so loving to mortals,

is trying to break through
the black sky
to shine her light on battlements broken
and towers fallen
and people forlorn,
just to watch
the deathly destruction
of Ilium,
and its ruin.

CHORUS LEADER: Once all the gods loved us!

CHORUS: Time was I dreamed
of a Trojan king
riding in a golden chariot
drawn by four immortal horses
flying to the stars!

(*in unison*)
How high were our hopes!

CHORUS LEADER: Suddenly
the gods withdrew their love,
and everything changed.

CHORUS: Trojan women weep
for husbands and brothers,
and children weep
for fathers and mothers
they never again will see.

(*in unison*)
The Greek spear
has destroyed
the land of Priam.

CHORUS LEADER: (*from the top of the ruin, seeing*
MENELAUS *coming from the direction of the*
sea)

But look! Menelaus himself,
the Greek king, is coming!
(*recoiling with the members of the* CHORUS
to the periphery)

MENELAUS: (*entering upstage from behind and
over the crest of the ruin from the direction
of the sea, preceded by two* SOLDIERS;
*dressed like a king in royal purple, but
wearing a scabbard containing a sword;
standing at the top of the ruin*)

860   How bright the sun will shine today
the moment Helen once more
belongs to me!

(*descending, prancing and swaggering
around the stage; his* SOLDIERS *stationing
themselves on the ruin*)
You know who I am!
Menelaus,
the king,
the general,
the man wronged many times.

I came to Troy with the Greek army,
not so much, as people think,
to get Helen
but *to get* Paris,
the man who was a guest in my home
and betrayed me, his host.
Paris! the thief who feasted at my table,
then stole my wife away!

Now, thanks to the gods,
he has paid the price,
along with his country.
He has fallen to the Greek spear
and lies in the dust—
trampled under horses' hooves—

as does his land around him.

This is the moment I've been waiting for:
to take back my wife!
She is here with the Trojan women
in this prisoner-of-war camp.
My fellow Greeks,
who fought to win her back,
have given her to me
to kill—
or, if I prefer,
to take her back alive
to the land of Argos.

I have decided
not to concern myself now
with things she did at Troy,
and not to kill her here,
but to take her back to Greece
in a seagoing ship with swift oars.

Once there I shall put her to death,
in as cruel a way as they
whose sons died because of her
may devise—
retribution for all my comrades
fallen at Troy.

(*to his* SOLDIERS)

880   All right, men!
Go to her tent and bring her out!
Drag her by her beautiful hair
rinsed in blood!
And when the winds are fair,
we shall take her back to Greece.

(*The* SOLDIERS *run to* HELEN*'s tent and enter it.*)

HECUBA: (*facing heaven*)

O Zeus,
You uphold the earth
and yet your throne is in highest heaven!
Whoever you are,
you are difficult to find,
and beyond man's comprehension.
Are you the inexorable laws of nature
or only a figment of man's imagination?

Does it matter?

I call upon you and praise you
and offer prayers to you,
but you pay no attention to me.
In silence you do as you please,
directing the affairs of men—
accomplishing *Justice*
in the end.

MENELAUS: What is this?
How strange and new this prayer
to the gods!

HECUBA: (*walking toward* MENELAUS)
Menelaus, you plan to kill her?
You really do?
Well, that is a good plan,
and I approve.

But don't set eyes on her,
for she will snare you
and conquer you
by seizing you with desire.
She captures the eyes
of the strongest of men
and steals their power,
ruining them and their cities, too.
She sets men on fire
and ends up burning down their houses!

This enchantress, so powerful,
is like a cup of poison.

(MENELAUS *sits on the block.*)

You and I know this well.
We have suffered because of her,
and so have many others
who now lie dead.

(*From the most upstage tent emerges* HELEN, *flirting with the* SOLDIERS, *who are gently escorting her. Unlike the* CHORUS, *she is beautifully dressed in a crimson gown in perfect condition and is adorned with jewelry; her mask is golden. Suddenly seeing* MENELAUS, *she pretends the* SOLDIERS *are manhandling her, and begins to struggle with them.* MENELAUS' *and* HELEN's *eyes meet.* MENELAUS, *gasping and gulping, stands.*)

HELEN: Menelaus, this is a frightful beginning,
              to be forcibly dragged out here
              by these strong-armed bullies
              you call soldiers!
              You seem to hate me.
              So, what have you decided?
900   Am I to live or die?

MENELAUS: I haven't yet made up my mind,
                    but the whole army
                    delivered you to me,
                    whom you wronged,
                    to put to death.

HELEN: (*running to* MENELAUS)
              I think I am entitled
              to say a word in my defense
              and show how unjust it would be
              to execute me—

for I am innocent!
I have been wronged!

MENELAUS: I came here to kill you,
not to hear you give a speech!

HECUBA: You must hear her out, Menelaus!
She cannot die
without the right of defending herself!

However,
after she has spoken,
give me the right of responding.
You know nothing of the crimes
she committed in Troy.
A complete hearing
can only end in her death.

MENELAUS: (*prancing about* HELEN, *gawking,
stroking his beard*)
This means delay
because it will take time
and a lot of breath.
But all right.
If she wishes to speak, she may.
It is only because of you, Hecuba,
and what you've said
that I grant her this privilege,
and not because she deserves it.

HELEN: (*standing; to* HECUBA *and to* MENELAUS)
How can I expect fair treatment
from either of you,
when both of you find me guilty
before I've said a word?
Even so,
I shall defend myself
and accuse those
who are truly to blame.

(MENELAUS, *like a judge, sits down upon
the block, rapt by the ensuing dialogue.*)

First, who began these evils?
(*pointing to* HECUBA, *accusingly*)
This old woman here!
It was *you*, (*pointing to* HECUBA *again*)
because you gave birth to Paris,
the cause of all our troubles!

920   Second, who was guilty after you?
The old king, Priam, your husband!
He ruined Troy, and he ruined me
by not destroying Paris in his infancy
as the oracle warned him to do!

Third, learn what happened next:
Three goddesses,
Athena, Hera, and Aphrodite,
held a beauty contest
in the sacred groves on Mount Ida.

It was our bad luck
that of all the men on earth
they chose Paris to judge
the most beautiful of the three.

All three goddesses
tampered with the outcome—
all three bribed the judge.

Athena's gift to Paris,
if he declared her fairest,
was that he would conquer Greece
as head of the Trojan army.
He should have chosen *her*!

Hera promised Paris,

if he judged her fairest,
that he would rule over
all Europe and Asia.
He should have chosen *her*!

Aphrodite,
who admired my beauty greatly,
(*patting her hair*)
promised Paris,
if he chose her
over the other two goddesses,
that she would give him
the most beautiful woman
in all the world—
(*proudly, flirtatiously*)
me!

(*to* HECUBA)
Well, your son Paris—the fool!—
like most foolish men,
chose Aphrodite.
The Goddess of Love won!

(*to* MENELAUS)
But even so,
Aphrodite's victory,
which resulted in the marriage
of Paris and me,
brought great good to Greece,
did it not?
Greece has won the Trojan War,
and you are not under the rule
of barbarians.
Things have gone well for Greece.
You are the victors!

(*to* ALL)
But Greece's victory
has ruined me.

I was used for my beauty,
and now I am reviled by the Greeks,
from whom I ought to receive a crown.
Instead, I am taken prisoner—
only to be killed.

(*to* MENELAUS)
I know what you are thinking—
that I should get to the point.
You are wondering,
why did I leave your palace
in the darkest hours of morning,
secretly, and fly?
I'll tell you why!

Paris—
(*pointing to* HECUBA)
this woman's son!—
on that night when he came to me,
slipped into my bed
940   with the Goddess of Love,
Aphrodite herself,
at his side.

And *you*—(*pointing to* MENELAUS)
unfaithful husband!—
were nowhere to be found!
You left me all alone with him
while *you*—
irresponsible man!—
went sailing off to Crete!

I ask myself,
what was I thinking
when I left my home and land
and everything I loved
and followed that stranger—that *Trojan*!—
from my comfortable life in Greece,
betraying my palace and my country?

Do not blame me!
Blame the goddesses
and their silly beauty contest!
If anyone should be punished,
punish Aphrodite!

And then you will become
more powerful than Zeus,
who rules the other gods
but who himself
is ruled by the Goddess of Love
and is her obedient slave.
Punish Aphrodite and forgive me!

If everything I've already said
hasn't convinced you,
what I'm about to say
surely will!

When Paris at last was killed in battle,
and my marriage arranged by the gods
no longer existed,
and I had to sleep *all alone* in my bed,
what did I do?

I should have left my palace in Troy
and run as quickly as I could
to the Greek ships.

Well, that's *exactly* what I tried to do,
on many occasions!
I have witnesses!
Ask the men who served as sentries
on Troy's towers and ramparts!

They will tell you how often
they discovered me
secretly trying to lower myself

down to the ground
from the high battlements,
with a rope around my waist.

960

Dear husband, as you believe in justice,
how can you even consider killing me?
What good will it do
to get revenge on me
for your past feelings of pain,
resentment for a wife
who left you,
driven by the storms of fate?
Put aside your feelings
and consider the facts!

Paris kidnapped me
and forced me to marry him.
My life here in Troy was without joy.
I lived here in misery.

And my predicament
has now resulted in my slavery
instead of bringing me the crown.

And my beauty, which is my glory,
what good is it to me now?
What good will it ever be again,
if you kill me to punish me
for what the gods have done?

Do you intend, in killing me,
to set yourself above the gods?
That would be a silly thing to do.

I have nothing more to say.

CHORUS LEADER: Hecuba, my queen,
defend your children and your country,
and break her spell!

CHORUS: (*in unison*)
> Her persuasive words
> are full of guile.

CHORUS LEADER: It is frightening
> how she turns all her guilt
> into innocence.

HECUBA: First, I must defend the goddesses—
> even though they have been on her side,
> not ours.
> I shall show her for the liar that she is.

> I do not believe that Hera, the wife of Zeus,
> and Athena, the daughter of Zeus,
> ever worked themselves
> into such a state of madness
> that Hera was willing
> to give Argos, *her* beloved city,
> or the virgin Athena
> to give Athens, *her* beloved city,
> to Paris,
> thus to enslave two favorite Greek cities
> by Trojan "barbarians"!

> The three goddesses
> did not come to Mount Ida
> for frivolous games
> and an outrageous
> beauty contest.
> (*contemptuously*)
> A beauty contest for goddesses!

> Why would the goddess Hera
> be taken with a sudden whim
> to be concerned with her own beauty?
> Was she looking to catch a husband
> better than Zeus?

And would Athena
want a wedding
given by the gods
when she was so afraid
of men and marriage
980   that she begged from her father Zeus
one gift only,
perpetual virginity?
She wanted to win a beauty contest?
She suddenly decided
she wanted to catch a man or a god
in marriage?

(*to* HELEN)
Do not make the goddesses out
to be crazy fools
to disguise your own heart's
evil intentions!
No, do not paint the gods of heaven
as stupid brutes and cruel!

Your arguments are transparent,
and anyone with any sense
can see right through them.

You claim—I have to laugh at it!—
that Aphrodite brought my son Paris
to Menelaus' palace in a ship.
And that she brought him to your bed.

That is ridiculous!
Had the goddess wished it,
she could have wafted you to Troy—
and a thousand more just like you!—
simply by wishing it,
while remaining quietly in heaven.

Now you shall learn the truth.

Paris, my son, was exceedingly beautiful,
more than any other man.

The moment you laid eyes on him,
you fell madly in love with him,
and it was as simple as that!
No need to invoke Aphrodite!
No need to invoke a goddess,
but you have invoked *three*!

All acts of human rashness
are blamed on the Goddess of Love!
"Aphrodite made me do it!" people say.

No! It was *not* the goddess!
You took one look at Paris—
resplendent in clothing from the east,
gleaming with gold—
and a fire kindled in your breast
that all the waters of the world
could not put out!

Moreover, not satisfied
with what you had
in your husband's palace in Greece,
you saw that wings had come
to carry you off to wealthy Troy—
that city *flooded* with gold!—
where you could try
to gratify your insatiable needs!
Here, you thought,
you could wallow in wealth,
and your extravagance could run wild!
Menelaus' house did not have enough
for your luxurious tastes.

Well now, you say,
my son *dragged* you away by force.

What nonsense!
How come no one knows of it?
What witnesses do you have?
Did you cry out for help?
If so,
why did no one in all of Greece
hear you?

1000   Your own brothers,
Castor and Pollux,
the twins, the *gemini*—
not yet among the stars—
were guests in Menelaus' palace
at the same time as Paris,
and they never reported hearing
so much as a peep out of you!

And after you came to Troy,
and the Greeks followed you here,
and the murderous battle of spears began,
whenever you heard news
that Menelaus' side was winning,
you would say,
"What a wonderful man Menelaus is!"
to torment Paris, my son, and to show
you were not truly committed to him.

But whenever the Trojans were winning,
suddenly
Menelaus meant nothing at all to you.

You were always for the winning side,
whichever it was,
and it was always changing.
It was not a question of right or wrong
but only what was best for you!

You say you let yourself secretly down
from the ramparts with a rope
like a desperate prisoner.

When were you ever discovered like that?
When were you ever brought before me
with a rope around your waist?
Too bad no one ever found you
with a rope around your neck!
or with your hand holding a knife
to your breast,
which are ways
many honorable women choose,
missing a former husband.

Then, too,
I told you what to do
time and time again.
I would say to you,
"Helen, go! Go, my daughter!
Go on your way! Go back to the Greeks!
Don't worry!
My son will make another marriage.
I myself shall conduct you
to the Greek ships.
Just give us peace at last.
Put an end to this war!"

But you did not like to hear such words.
You said to me,
"Mind your own business, old woman!"

1020   You had a great time in Paris' palace,
spoiled by the luxury,
and you enjoyed the "barbarians"
prostrating themselves before your feet,
worshipping you.
You liked that enormously!

And after all that has happened,
now you come out here all dressed up,
wearing a gorgeous gown and jewelry!

Is this the proper way
to greet your husband
under the circumstances?

You do not deserve
to breathe the same air as he,
you despicable creature!

It would have been more fitting
had you come out humbly,
in rent robes, in rags, trembling with fear,
your head shorn.
That is the way you should have come
to greet him,
showing shame and remorse at last.
That would have been more appropriate
than persisting in your brazenness
after all the evil things you've done.

(*to* MENELAUS)
Menelaus, great King,
one more word from me,
and I'm finished.

Crown Greece with honor.
Kill this woman!
That would be an act worthy of you.
Establish this precedent for all women
for all time.
*Death to the woman
who betrays her husband*!

(MENELAUS *stands.*)

CHORUS LEADER: Menelaus, King,
         son of the House of Atreus!
         Act in a manner worthy of your house
         and your ancestors!
         The Greeks say you are a woman—

all teats!
Kill this woman,
and even your enemies
will call you a great man!

MENELAUS: (*to the* CHORUS LEADER *and to* HECUBA)
I see things just as you do!
This woman left my home
to go to a stranger's bed
because she wanted to.
She made up the story
of the beauty contest
to put the blame on Aphrodite.

(*to* HELEN)
Go and find those who will stone you
and instantly pay the price
1040   for the long sufferings of the Greeks!
Die!
And dishonor me no more!

HELEN: (*groveling; kneeling and embracing his knees*)
No, great King!
At your knees, I beg you,
do not attribute to me
evil that comes from the gods.
Do not kill me!
Have mercy!
Forgive me!

HECUBA: (*to* MENELAUS)
Do not betray all the men she slaughtered,
many of them your friends!
Do not forget them!
I implore you on their behalf
and on behalf of their children.
Do not betray them!

MENELAUS: (*to* HECUBA)
      Be quiet, old woman!
      I am not listening to her!
      She means nothing to me!

      (*to his* SOLDIERS)
      Men, take her to our ship!
      Guard her until we sail!

(*The* SOLDIERS *walk to* HELEN. *Each one takes her by an arm, but the ensuing dialogue prevents them from advancing.*)

HECUBA: Do not sail on the same ship as she!

MENELAUS: Why not?
      Has she gained weight?

HECUBA: Once a lover, always a lover!

MENELAUS: Not necessarily!
      But it shall be as you wish!
      She will not board the same ship as I.
      Your advice is good.

      (*He nods to his* SOLDIERS. *The* SOLDIERS *begin to lead* HELEN *downstage right in the direction of the harbor. She moves slowly and seductively.*)

And when she arrives in Greece,
this wicked woman
will die a horrible death,
as she deserves.
She will inspire all women
to be faithful to their husbands,
which is not an easy thing to do.
Her death will scare away
the stupid ideas of women

even more depraved than she.

(*Just before* HELEN *exits, she breaks free of the* SOLDIERS *and runs into* MENELAUS' *receptive arms. They kiss passionately.   The* SOLDIERS *come back for her and look at* MENELAUS, *who nods.   Again they escort her downstage right.   Just before exiting, she turns and gives* MENELAUS *a flirtatious smile, batting her eyes.* MENELAUS *sighs as she exits.   He pauses a moment, stroking his beard, then immediately exits downstage right following her, first walking, then running.*)

1060   CHORUS LEADER: (*facing heaven*)
           O Zeus,
           you are god of both Troy and Greece.
           When you betray Troy,
           how can Greece ever trust you again?

       CHORUS: Gone now is your temple in Ilium
               and its altar,
               fragrant with sacrificial incense—
               burning barley and smoke of myrrh
               filling the air of the city
               and rising
               to the glades of Mount Ida.

               Ida!—where wild ivy grows,
               and rivers run with melting snows,
               and on whose radiant and holy peak
               the dawn's first light appears and glows.

               Gone are your sacrifices
               and the festivals
               lasting all through the night
               with choirs singing—
               how sweet and joyful the sounds!—
               and young women dancing
               under the stars in the moonlight,

and prayers chanted,
and golden images worshipped.
Gone!

(*in unison*)
Gone,
all things sacred to Trojans!

CHORUS LEADER: I wonder, O Zeus, our Lord,
          whether you even care
          about such things
          as you sit upon your heavenly throne
          high up in the skies!

CHORUS: (*in unison*)
          Do you care
          that my city is perishing?

CHORUS LEADER: Do you watch
1080   as fire destroys her?

CHORUS: O dearest husband,
          your spirit wanders about
          unable to find peace
          because your dead body
          lies unburied.

          A swift-winging ship
          will carry me over the sea
          to Argos,
          where horses graze
          and men live within sky-towering walls
          made of great stone blocks,
          walls built by giants.

          I saw
          a crowd of frightened Trojan children
          standing at the city gates.
          A little girl was crying through her tears,

"Mama,
the Greeks are taking me away from you,
all alone, to their big black ships!"

Are they taking them to Salamis,
the immortal island with holy temples,
or to the mountain peaks
of the Corinthian isthmus,
where Pelops once was king?

1100   Menelaus is sending me
weeping from Troy,
away from my country,
to be a Greek slave!

Well, while Menelaus' ship
sails on the high seas,
flying on the Aegean,

(*cursing*)
May Zeus hurl lightning,
white and jagged,
casting wild sea light,
and may it strike his ship!

[77-84][4]   May Zeus turn the skies pitch black
and send down torrential rain,
hailstones as large as rocks,
and blazing thunderbolts
to set the ships afire!

May he send a howling hurricane
to churn the deep,
creating monstrous waves
and whirlpools!

May Zeus and Poseidon
make the Aegean Sea rage
and crash against the rocky reefs

and promontories
to fill every sheltering bay
with the bodies of dead Greeks!

(*mocking*)
While on a tempest-tossed ship,
I can just see Helen,
who is, after all, the daughter of Zeus,
calmly sitting and admiring herself
in a large mirror with a golden frame,
the kind of mirror
young girls love so much.

(*cursing*)
May Menelaus and Helen
never get home again
to see the sands of the Spartan shore,
his ancestral home,
nor the magnificent temple of Athena
with its bronze doors,
nor the tombs
where his ancestors dwell!

(*in unison*)
Through a disastrous marriage to Paris,
Helen brought shame to mighty Greece
and suffering to the shores of Troy.

CHORUS LEADER: (*looking toward the city gates; in
        shock*)
        Look!
        Wave upon wave of grief!
        (ALL *look.*)

(TALTHYBIUS *approaches slowly from the city gate.
Behind him are his two* SOLDIERS, *bearing Hector's
shield horizontally between them, the lead* SOLDIER
facing forward, the aft SOLDIER *also facing forward. Lying on the shield is the dead* ASTYANAX,

*washed clean, naked except for a loincloth, head
turned upstage.   The* SOLDIERS *stop stage center
while* TALTHYBIUS *walks toward the tents stage
right, then turns and watches.*)

CHORUS LEADER: Unhappy Trojan women,
1120   look on the body of Astyanax, our prince,
                 whom the Greeks have murdered
                 by flinging him from the city wall
                 with no more concern
                 than if they were throwing a ball!

CHORUS: (*in unison*)
                 Who has heard
                 of such cruelty?

TALTHYBIUS: (*to* HECUBA)
                 Hecuba,
                 the last of Pyrrhus' ships
                 is being loaded with spoils.

                 Pyrrhus himself has already sailed
                 on an earlier ship,
                 Andromache with him.
                 I could see her weeping on the deck
                 through my own hot tears,
                 which I could not contain
                 when I heard her mourning Troy
                 and saying her last good-bye
                 to Hector's grave.

                 She begged Pyrrhus, Achilles' son,
                 to arrange for the burial of Astyanax,
                 your grandchild
                 and Hector's son,
                 who lost his life
                 when he was flung
                 from the top of the city walls.

(*pointing to the shield bearing the corpse*)
And here is Hector's bronze-backed shield
the one he used in battle
to guard his own body,
the same shield that struck terror
in Greek hearts.

Andromache, the mother of the dead boy,
sent it from the ship
in my care.
She pleaded with Achilles' son
not to take it back to Greece,
where it would be
a constant reminder of her past grief,
and not to place it in the very room
where, on a Greek bed,
she would have to make love.

1140   She requested that the child
be buried on the shield
in a simple grave—
not in a cedarwood coffin
placed in a stone tomb.

She begged Pyrrhus to order
that the dead child
be given to you,
to lay in your arms to wash,
to place in a shroud,
to adorn with a crown and flowers,
insofar as you had the strength
and the necessary materials.
These things she requested of you
because she was unable
to bury the boy herself.

As soon as you have prepared the body
with robes and flowers and a crown,
we will bury him,

and then the ships can sail.

Do what you have been asked to do
as quickly as you can.

One task I spared you.
As I was crossing
nearby Scamander's stream,
I washed the body in its waters
and cleansed the wounds.

Now I am going
to break the ground
and dig the grave,
so that you and I,
by working together,
may more quickly set the ships
on their long voyage home.
(*departing stage right in the direction of
the harbor*)

HECUBA: (*to the two* SOLDIERS *carrying Hector's
shield with the dead* ASTYANAX *on it*)
Set Hector's shield upon the ground!

(*The* SOLDIERS *set down the shield with the
corpse of* ASTYANAX *and withdraw to the
ruin.* HECUBA *moves stage center, just upstage of the shield and corpse.*)
What a painful and bitter sight!

O Greeks, your spears are cold,
but your hearts are colder—
to perpetrate a murder
the likes of which
the world has never known!

Did you fear this child?[5]
What a strange murder for brave men!

1160   Were you afraid
           he might rebuild Troy one day?
           Have you no pride?

           I thought you conquered us
           by your great strength.
           But now, despite so many thousands
           of Trojans dead
           by Greek spears,
           and Ilium laid low,
           and everything Trojan lost,
           I see how really weak you were:
           You were afraid of a little boy!

           I despise the fear that comes
           when reason flies away.
           Even fear must be based on reason.

           (*kneeling, then speaking to the corpse*)
           Oh, my dearest child,
           what a cruel and horrible death
           came to you!

           If you had grown to manhood
           and died for Troy in battle,
           if you had known the joy of love
           and marriage
           and had ruled your kingdom
           in glorious majesty,
           we would have called you blessed.

           How foolish of me
           to even think of blessedness now.

           Ah, you were too young
           to expect or imagine such things,
           although they were part of your heritage.

           Poor little one!

How brutally our ancient walls,
built by gods,
(*gently brushing the head with her fingertips*)
have smashed your little head!—
the curls that your mother tended
like flowers in a garden,
and the rosy cheeks, which she kissed,
where now the ghastly white
and jagged bone grins . . .
(*averting her eyes*)
I cannot bear to look any more!

(*after a moment, examining the corpse's hands*)
Your hands,
how sweetly like your father's they are;
how loosely now they fall!

(*caressing the lips with her fingertips*)
Dear lips that once made great promises
doomed never to be fulfilled.
How many times
you jumped into my bed at daybreak
and promised,
"Grandma, when you die,
I will cut off a thick lock of my hair,
and I shall have a parade
and bring lots of my friends
and visit your grave
and tell you how much I love you
and good-bye."

You have cheated me!
You are not burying me,
but I you, poor boy,
while you are still so young,
and I am now so old,
a very old woman without a nation

1180

and without one child left!
I am burying *you*!
And *my* tears flow,
not *yours*!

How you would run to greet me!
How welcome the patter of those little feet!
And you would climb up into my lap . . .
all those hugs and kisses! . . .
and so sweet to watch you sleeping. . . .

All over!

What would a poet write
as an epitaph for you?

"Here lies a child
whom the Greeks murdered
because they feared him."

Ah! Now *that* is something
for the Greeks to boast about,
and all of Greece to take pride in!

Child, they have taken everything from us!
Only one thing have they left,
your father's shield.
It is yours!
You have won his bronze shield,
even though you could not win
his heritage.

(*lovingly fingering the shield*)
O shield that protected Hector,
you could not protect him well enough,
even though he looked after you so well.

(*fingering the handle and making a pleasant discovery*)

Look here!
How sweet
the imprint of his hand
upon the handle!

(*fingering the rim and making another
pleasant discovery*)
And here!
How sweet
the stains of his sweat
on your well-turned rim,
the sweat that
in the thick of battle
rolled in beads
from Hector's brow and beard,
drop after drop
falling on the brim.

(*to the* CHORUS)
Come, Trojan women,
give me anything you have
to serve as an adornment
for this pitiful body.

(*to the corpse*)
Fate has not given us much
to make a fine display.
But you shall have whatever we have.

(*to the* CHORUS *and the audience*)
Anyone who imagines he has security
because he prospers,
and who rejoices in his prosperity,
is a fool.

Our fortunes have a way of leaping about
in different directions
like a lunatic dancing in the wind.
And no one is fortunate

1200

just because
he has good fortune now.

(HECUBA *remains kneeling before the corpse.
Meanwhile the members of the* CHORUS *have been
examining their bodies for suitable decoration.
The* CHORUS LEADER *removes her shawl.   The one*
WOMAN *with a gold bracelet—a solid circular
bangle—removes it. A third* WOMAN *picks some of
the wildflowers.   Then all three* WOMEN *walk to*
HECUBA *to deliver their gifts.*)

CHORUS LEADER: (*giving the shawl*)
          Here, Hecuba.
          This is all we have.

WOMAN: (*giving the bunch of wildflowers*)
          —nothing the Greeks wanted for spoils.

WOMAN: (*giving the bracelet*)
          —adornments for your grandson's body.

HECUBA: (*receiving and setting the gifts on the
          ground, then speaking to the corpse*)
          My child, these are not trophies
          of your victories over your companions
          in competitions of chariot or horse races
          or games of bows and arrows
          that your grandmother,
          your father's mother,
          is going to lay upon you,
          not precious things
          from possessions once your own.

          But this is all we have.
          Helen, hated by God,
          has stolen everything precious from you—
          your robes, your crown, your life—
          and she has destroyed your nation.

CHORUS LEADER: (*kneeling before the corpse*)
> My heart is breaking because of you.
> I hoped one day you'd be
> a great lord in our nation.

HECUBA: (*ceremoniously holding up the shawl,
> then draping the body with it*)
> I place upon you

1220
> the glory of Trojan robes,
> which you should have worn
> on your wedding day
> to a beautiful princess from the East.

> (*ceremoniously holding up the bracelet,
> then setting it on the center of the shawl*)
> O beloved shield of Hector,
> glorious in battle,
> receive this crown,
> in recognition
> of ten thousand victories won.

> (*ceremoniously holding up a single wild-
> flower, then placing it on the bracelet*)
> Dead shield with dead body,
> yet you are deathless!
> For so long as
> there are people upon the earth,
> they shall tell this story,
> and you shall be remembered.

CHORUS LEADER: O Hector,
> O bearer of this great shield,
> behold how the earth
> shall receive your dear child!

CHORUS: (*in unison, to* HECUBA)
> Mother of sorrows,
> sing a song of death!

HECUBA: Woe, woe!

CHORUS LEADER: A dirge for all our dead!

HECUBA: Sorrow!

CHORUS LEADER: Sorrow true,
sorrow infinite,
sorrow never to be forgotten!

HECUBA: (*to the corpse*)
My darling,
I have covered your wounds
like a physician,
but even a physician
cannot restore you to life.

Your father will comfort you
and take care of you now.

CHORUS LEADER: (*wailing*)
Strike your head
over and over again,
and clap your hands
to the rhythm of moving oar blades.
Ee! Oh! Oh! Oh!

(*The* CHORUS *forms a circle that moves around the corpse and* HECUBA *slowly once or twice. Each member of the* CHORUS *rhythmically strikes her forehead, then claps her hands three times as she circles. When this mourning dance is over, the circle breaks downstage and the members of the* CHORUS *end up standing in a row, shoulder-to-shoulder just behind and upstage of* HECUBA.)

HECUBA: Dearest Trojan women,
the gods . . . (*breaking off abruptly*)

CHORUS LEADER: Hecuba,
what do you want to tell us?

CHORUS: What are you thinking?

You can tell us anything.

What were you going to say?

1240   HECUBA: The gods amount to nothing after all.
What do they care of my suffering?
They love to beat me.
This they do quite well.

They are consumed
with their hatred of Troy.
My prayers and my sacrifices
have been useless.

And yet,
if God was not tormenting us,
and torturing us,
and dashing us to the ground,
no one would ever hear of us.
We would remain unsung forever
instead of giving everlasting themes
in poetry and music
to future generations.

(*Each* WOMAN *takes a wildflower from*
HECUBA*'s bunch and places it on the shawl*
covering the corpse.)

(HECUBA *to the* SOLDIERS; *kindly*)
Go now,
and bury the boy in his poor grave.
He has such garlands
as befit the dead,

although I think
it makes little difference to them
whether they are decorated or not.
This is merely an empty gesture
to satisfy the vanity of the living.

(*The two* SOLDIERS *lift the shield bearing the corpse and then freeze.*)

CHORUS LEADER: Forlorn mother,
with great hopes torn asunder!

CHORUS: How many smiled at this child's birth!

He was born yesterday in happiness
and with everything!

(*in unison*)
And today he has died grimly
and with nothing!

(*The* SOLDIERS *bearing the shield exit slowly downstage right toward the harbor. There is no movement onstage until the corpse and retinue are out of sight. Then* TALTHYBIUS *enters, returning over the ruin from the direction of the sea. He stops at the crest and gazes at* HECUBA, *while the* CHORUS *notices something out of view high on the city walls, above the entrance to the city.*)

CHORUS LEADER: Look up there!
Who are the men I see
on top of the walls,
waving fiery torches?

CHORUS: (*in unison*)
Men waving torches
means new agony for Troy.

TALTHYBIUS: (*looking up, creating a megaphone
with his hands, and shouting*)
1260   Hallooo, you captains up there!
Your orders are to set fire
to the city of Priam!
Well, what are you waiting for?
Why are you still holding the torches?
Toss the fires into the city immediately!
Once the city is leveled,
our work is done—
and we can joyfully sail for home!

(*to the* CHORUS, *in a normal voice*)
And you, Trojan women,
pay attention
so I don't have to repeat myself.
When the trumpet sounds,
start moving
toward the Greek ships
in which you sail from Troy.

(*Two* SOLDIERS *of Ulysses appear from the
direction of the harbor; to* HECUBA)

Hecuba,
these men, sent by Ulysses,
have come for you.
You are sailing from Troy on his ship,
to be his slave,
most unfortunate of women.

HECUBA: Ah, I am miserable
beyond measure!
This is now the end.
This is the peak of all my suffering.
I am leaving my country, my city,
its streets all aflame.

Come, old feet,

bear me a little closer to the walls
that I may salute my city
before she falls.

(*She takes two steps toward the walls but is
stopped when the flames from the burning
city suddenly grow brighter, as indicated
by the upstage segment of the wall turning
blood red and by flickering flames reflecting on* HECUBA. TALTHYBIUS *walks toward
the city gates, then turns to face* HECUBA,
and stations himself between the gates and
HECUBA.)

(*facing the walls,* HECUBA *continues*)
O Troy,
once so great
among the non-Greek nations!
Now your very name,
which the whole world knew,
will be stolen from you.
They are burning you
and they are dragging us
away as slaves.

(*hands and face toward heaven*)
O gods! Merciful gods!
(*hands and face dropping*)
But why pray to the gods?
They do not listen to our prayers.

Come, let us rush back into the city!
O Troy, your agony is my own!
I want to die with you!

(*She tries to run in the direction of the city
gates, but* TALTHYBIUS *blocks her.*)

TALTHYBIUS: Your suffering

1280

has driven you out of your mind,
poor woman.

(*to the two* SOLDIERS *of Ulysses*)
Men, lead her to your ship at once
and hand deliver her to Ulysses.
She is his *prize*.

(*The two* SOLDIERS *start to escort* HECUBA *stage right in the direction of the harbor, each* SOLDIER *taking her by an elbow. But her arms, slipping from their grip, slowly stretch to heaven. The* SOLDIERS *drop their arms, stop walking, and gaze at her.*)

HECUBA: Oh! Oh! Oh!
(*hands and face to heaven*)
O God,
Ruler of our nation!
You begot us,
O Father, our King!
It is we, your children!
Do you not see how we suffer?
We do not deserve this!

CHORUS LEADER: He sees but does not care.

CHORUS: The land dies.

The greatest of cities perishes.

(*in unison*)
Ilium is no more.

HECUBA: All Troy is burning:
the citadel, the towers, the homes. . . .

CHORUS LEADER: Our nation,
fallen to spear and fire,

1300

dissolves into nothingness,
goes up in smoke
that soars to heaven
on the wings of the wind.

HECUBA: O land that nurtured my children!

CHORUS LEADER: Alas!

HECUBA: (*in a trance*)
O children, hear me!
Your mother is calling you!

CHORUS LEADER: You cry to the dead.
They do not hear.

HECUBA: (*sinking to her knees, then beating the earth*)
I sink to the ground
and beat the earth with my fists.

CHORUS LEADER: (*also sinking to her knees, then beating the earth*)
I, too, kneel to the earth
and call out to loved ones
in the underworld.

HECUBA: We are being taken . . .

CHORUS: (*in unison*)
You hear the cry of pain!

HECUBA: . . . taken away
to the house of bondage!

CHORUS LEADER: . . . taken away
from our homeland!

HECUBA: O Priam, my husband,

> without a loved one to dig your grave!
> You are dead and know nothing
> of my destruction.

CHORUS LEADER: Dark death came
> and closed Priam's eyes.

CHORUS: He was so good,

> and he was murdered so maliciously.

(*The sea and sky are turning bright orange-red.*)

HECUBA: O temples of the gods!
> O nation that I love!

CHORUS: (*in unison*)
> Alas!

HECUBA: You are killed by the red flame
> that follows the red spear.

CHORUS LEADER: O Troy!
> Soon you will fall to earth
> and disappear,
> and men will forget your name.

(*A strong wind comes up and continues to the end
of the play.   The sea and sky grow brighter orange-red.*)

HECUBA: (*standing*)
> My home vanishes
1320 > in dust and ash and smoke
> winging to the sky.

CHORUS LEADER: (*standing*)
> Its very name
> will vanish, too.

CHORUS: Sooner or later all things disappear,

one after another!

(*in unison*)
Now it is Ilium's turn.

(*In the distance, a short, cascading rumbling is heard.*)

HECUBA: Do you hear?

Do you know what it means?

CHORUS LEADER: Yes,
it is the sound of towers falling.

HECUBA: The earth trembles,
shaking the whole city
and the plain beyond.

CHORUS LEADER: The earthquake
engulfs everything . . .

(*Suddenly all rumbling stops.*)

CHORUS LEADER: . . . and passes on.

(*From the direction of the harbor, the trumpet sounds* [ta RA tan ta RA].[6] ALL *momentarily freeze.*)

HECUBA: (*confidently*)
O gray spirit of a woman,
(*lifting her head high and commanding her limbs as if they were servants*)
O shaking and trembling limbs,
make your way

forward
into the new day
of slavery![7]

(HECUBA *marches one or two steps downstage right
toward the harbor behind the* SOLDIERS *of Ulysses
[the front guard], in single file.   The trumpet
sounds a second time as before;* ALL *momentarily
freeze.*)

CHORUS LEADER: Good-bye, dear city!
          Good-bye, dear country
          who nourished my children!

CHORUS: (*in unison*)
          Mourn the unhappiest city!

CHORUS LEADER: We must go and face
          whatever awaits us!
          Onward!
1332   To the Greek ships!

(*The* CHORUS *falls into single file behind* HECUBA *and the*
SOLDIERS *of Ulysses [the front guard].* TALTHYBIUS *and his*
SOLDIERS *[the rear guard] fall into single file behind the*
CHORUS, *and* ALL *march downstage right toward the harbor.*
    *The lighting starts to fade. Suddenly the flames of the
city momentarily grow exceedingly bright.*
    TALTHYBIUS *and his* SOLDIERS *stop, turn, and face the
conflagration, shielding their eyes.   Brightness slowly
fades and* ALL *resume their march. After* ALL *have exited, a
rumbling, cascading sound grows in intensity so that when
complete darkness comes, the sound is thunderous, ending
in a great crash. The wind howls and dies.*)

THE END

PRONUNCIATION GUIDE

∞∞∞∞∞∞∞∞

NOTES

∞∞∞∞∞∞∞∞

SELECTED SOURCES

PRONUNCIATION GUIDE

For American English Pronunciation of Greek Names

Accent the syllable in CAPITALS

Achilles	uh KIL leez
Aegean	ee JEE un
Agamemnon	a guh MEM non
Andromache	an DRAH muh kee
Aphrodite	af roh DY* tee
Apollo	uh POL loh
Argos	AR guss
Aristophanes	air iss TOF uh neez
Aristotle	AIR iss tot'l
Astyanax	uh STEE uh nax
Athena	uh THEE* nuh
Atreus	AY* tree uss

* in all cases:
y (vowel) as in *my*
th as in *thin*, not as in *this*
ay as in *day*

Cassandra	kuh SAN druh (*not* kuh SAHN druh)
Castor	KASS ter
Clytemnestra	kly tem NESS truh
Corinthian	kuh RIN thee un
Euripides	yoo RIP uh deez
Eurotas	yoo ROH tuss
Hector	HEK ter
Hecuba	HEK yoo buh
Helen	HEL un
Hera	HAIR uh
Ida	EYE duh
Ilium	IL ee um
Ionian	eye OH nee un
Iphigenia	if uh juh NY uh
Ithaca	ITH uh kuh
Menelaus	men uh LAY uss
Paris	PAIR iss
Pelops	PEL ups (*not* PEE lops)
Penelope	puh NEL uh pee

Pollux	POL lux
Polyxena	pol ee ZEE nuh (*not* pol LIX uh nuh)
Poseidon	poh SY dun
Priam	PRY um (*not* PREE um)
Pyrrhus	PIR uss
Salamis	SAL uh muss
Scamander	skuh MAN der
Sicily	SISS uh lee
Simois	SIM oh iss
Talthybius	tal THI bee uss
Thebes	THEEBZ
Thessaly	THESS uh lee
Trojan	TROH jun
Troy	TROY
Tyndareus	tin DAIR ee uss
Ulysses	yoo LISS eez
Zeus	ZOOSS

NOTES

[1] ll. 1–97 (p. 47) and other line numbers.

The numbers in the left margin of the script run from 1 through 1332 and are usually presented every twenty lines. They closely approximate the line numbers of the two Greek texts of *The Trojan Women* from which this adaptation was made, the "eclectic" text in the Loeb Classical Library and the "Oxford" text in Barlow (see Selected Sources 7 and 8). The line numbers enable readers of Greek to refer to the Greek texts. The line numbers do not correspond to lines in this English adaptation, should the reader count them, because Greek lines and English lines are not the same length.

The line numbers 1 through 97 are a special case. This large block of lines represents the entire Greek prologue, which spans those line numbers and which has been revised to form the Prologue in this English adaptation (see Introduction).

[2] l. 135. "Priam, the king, my husband, father of fifty boys" (p. 57).

According to Homer's *Iliad*, Priam was the father of fifty sons and twelve daughters. Hecuba bore him nineteen of those sons and several of his daughters (the exact number is unknown). He had other children by other women. Hecuba and Priam's children included Priam's most famous—his sons Hector and Paris and daughter Cassandra.

[3]   ll. 799–859 (pp. 119–22).

This choral ode has been revised. The line numbers, referring to the Greek text, are inclusive, like the line numbers in the Prologue, to show that the entire ode has been revised in this English adaptation (see Introduction).

[4]   ll. [77–84] (pp. 143–4).

The brackets around the line numbers indicate that this portion of text (from "May Zeus turn the skies pitch black" to "with the bodies of dead Greeks") has been moved from its original location in the Greek prologue to this new position following line 1106 in this choral ode. This passage, which concerns a storm at sea, has been revised in accordance with the context of this choral ode in this English adaptation (see Introduction).

[5]   ll. 1159–61. "Did you fear this child? What a strange murder for brave men! Were you afraid he might rebuild Troy one day?" (pp. 147–8).

Hecuba is ridiculing the Greeks for what she calls their unreasonable fear. However, earlier she had hoped that Astyanax would one day rebuild Troy, and she said so to Andromache: "Rear this boy . . . to manhood [and he] may one day rebuild Troy" (ll. 702–5, p. 106). Isn't Hecuba being hypocritical when she ridicules this Greek fear that earlier was her hope?

Human psychology is complex, and no one portrays its complexity better than Euripides. Perhaps Hecuba has changed her mind since the time when she was speaking to Andromache. By the time she is speaking to the Greeks, she has come to realize that Astyanax was after all only a little boy and therefore not a threat to the Greeks. Even if he lived to manhood his chances of rebuilding Troy were not great.

But even if Hecuba has not changed her mind, one can hardly accuse her of hypocrisy simply because one moment she is giving comfort to a loved one (Andromache) by means of a thought (Astyanax may one day rebuild

Troy) and subsequently she is trying to humiliate her enemy for acting on the same thought. Comforting a loved one is one of the few privileges left to the vanquished, and humiliating an enemy is one of the few weapons. For Euripides to have Hecuba both comfort and humiliate with the same words shows his genius.

6   ll. 1329 and 1331. "(*From the direction of the harbor, the trumpet sounds* [*ta RA tan ta RA*])" (p. 162).

The ancient Greek trumpet (*salpinx*) sounded more like a modern French horn or a hunting horn than a modern trumpet (16, track 1). The call has been rendered as "taratantara" (17, p. 120), the rhythm of which I have interpreted as above.

7   l. 1330. "forward into the new day of slavery!" (p. 163).

What happens to Hecuba after *The Trojan Women* ends? Earlier in the play, Cassandra, the oracle who always tells the truth, prophesies that Hecuba will not go with Ulysses on his ship but will die in Troy (ll. 428–30, p. 82). Hecuba's manner of death is not stated. Perhaps she is sitting on the beach, waiting to board Ulysses' ship, when a soldier, coming to fetch her, discovers that she is dead. Perhaps she deliberately drowns herself in Troy's harbor; she had said earlier that there are situations when it is appropriate for an honorable woman to commit suicide (ll. 1012–14, p. 137), and near the end of the play she tries to destroy herself by running into the burning city (ll. 1282–3, p. 158).

In another play by Euripides entitled *Hecuba*, Hecuba does not die in Troy. (The Greek playwrights felt no need for consistency among their own plays, even in their trilogies.) Hecuba sails as a slave from Troy to Thrace, not on Ulysses' ship but on Agamemnon's. In Thrace she learns of a prophecy of a Thracian oracle that states she will die of drowning while sailing from Thrace to Argos. It is not clear whether she will fall overboard or deliberately jump.

The two prophecies, Cassandra's in *The Trojan Women* and the Thracian oracle's in *Hecuba*, agree on one thing: Hecuba will never be a slave in Greece because she will never get there.

SELECTED SOURCES

1. Aeschylus. *Agamemnon: A Play*. Translated with introduction, notes, and synopsis by Howard Rubenstein. El Cajon, Calif.: Granite Hills Press™, 1998.

2. Aristophanes. *The Frogs*. In *Aristophanes II*, Loeb Classical Library, translated by Benjamin Bickley Rogers. Cambridge, Mass., and London: Harvard Univ. Press, 1924. Reprint, 1996. [Contains the Greek text.]

3. Aristophanes. *The Frogs*, translated by Gilbert Murray, and *The Acharnians*, anonymous translator. In *The Complete Greek Drama*, Vol. 2, edited by Whitney J. Oates and Eugene O'Neill, Jr. New York: Random House, 1938.

4. Aristotle. *Poetics*. In *Aristotle XXIII*, Loeb Classical Library, edited and translated by Stephen Halliwell. London: Duckworth, 1987. Cambridge, Mass., and London: Harvard Univ. Press, 1995.

5. Easterling, P. E., ed. *The Cambridge Companion to Greek Tragedy*. Cambridge: Cambridge Univ. Press, 1997.

6.   Easterling, P. E., and B. M. W. Knox, eds. *The Cambridge History of Classical Literature.* Vol. 1, Part 2 *Greek Drama.* Cambridge: Cambridge Univ. Press, 1989.

7.   Euripides. *The Daughters of Troy [The Trojan Women].* In *Euripides I,* Loeb Classical Library, translated by Arthur S. Way. Cambridge, Mass.: Harvard Univ. Press; London: Wm. Heinemann Ltd., 1912. Reprint, 1959. [Contains the "eclectic" Greek text of *The Trojan Women.*]

8.   Euripides. *[The] Trojan Women.* Translated and with commentary by Shirley A. Barlow. Warminster, England: Aris & Phillips Ltd., 1986. Fourth corrected impression, 1993. [Contains the "Oxford" Greek text of *The Trojan Women* © 1981.]

9.   Euripides. *The Trojan Women.* Translated by Gilbert Murray. In *The Complete Greek Drama,* Vol. 1, edited by Whitney J. Oates and Eugene O'Neill, Jr. New York: Random House, 1938.

10.   Euripides. *The Trojan Women.* In *Three Greek Plays: Prometheus Bound, Agamemnon, The Trojan Women,* The Norton Library, translated with introductions by Edith Hamilton. New York: W. W. Norton & Company, 1937. Reprint, 1958.

11.   Homer. *Iliad.* Loeb Classical Library, translated by A. T. Murray. Vol. 1. Cambridge, Mass.: Harvard Univ. Press; London: Wm. Heinemann Ltd., 1924. Reprint, 1960.

12.   Homer. *Iliad*. Loeb Classical Library, translated by A. T. Murray. Vol. 2. Cambridge, Mass.: Harvard Univ. Press; London: Wm. Heinemann Ltd., 1925. Reprint, 1957.

13.   Jebb, Richard C. "Euripides." In *Encyclopaedia Britannica*, 11th ed. Vol. 9. New York: Encyclopaedia Britannica Co., 1910.

14.   Kitto, H. D. F. *The Greeks*. Harmondsworth, England, and Baltimore: Penguin Books Ltd., 1951. Reprint, 1962.

15.   Murray, Gilbert. *Euripides and His Age*. Williams & Norgate, 1918. Reprint, with a new introduction by H. D. F. Kitto, London: Oxford Univ. Press, 1965.

16.   Neuman, Gayle Stuwe, Philip Neuman, and William Gavin. *Music of the Ancient Greeks*. Compact Sound Disc. Track 1: Salpinx call (fifth century B.C.). Pandourion Records U.S.A., 1997.

17.   West, M. L. *Ancient Greek Music*. Oxford: Oxford Univ. Press, Clarendon Paperback edition, 1994.